# My All, His All

# My All, His All

By

J. Edwin Orr, D.Phil. (Oxford), Ed.D. (UCLA)

Introduction by Billy Graham

Edited by Richard Owen Roberts

INTERNATIONAL
AWAKENING
PRESS

Wheaton, Illinois

1989

Published By

## INTERNATIONAL AWAKENING PRESS
Post Office Box 232
Wheaton, Illinois 60189 U.S.A.

**A Division Of**
**International Awakening Ministries, Inc.**

First Published as "Full Surrender"

1950

New and Revised Edition Copyright 1989

by

The Oxford Association for Research in Revival

All Rights Reserved

Printed in the United States of America

ISBN 0-926474-02-2

Library of Congress

Catalogue Card No. 89-83747

65,420

Dedicated to
the praying, giving people of
Providence Chapel

# Contents

# Introduction To the First Edition

## BY BILLY GRAHAM

Dr. J. Edwin Orr, in my opinion, is one of the greatest authorities on the history of religious revivals in the Protestant world. I think that God has given him one of the greatest and most unique ministries anywhere in the nation, and his contribution to the revival which I believe is on the way is invaluable. I know of no man who has a greater passion for worldwide revival or a greater love for the souls of men.

About fifteen years ago I first heard of Edwin Orr through his books. His books on faith were a tremendous blessing in my own life. Twelve years ago I met him in Florida for the first time and thus began an acquaintance which has ripened into warm friendship.

In 1947, during our evangelistic campaigns in Great Britain, I heard that Dr. Orr was engaged in research into the nineteenth-century awakenings, so I wrote him at Oxford University and afterwards spent half a day there, viewing the sights of the ancient city and making the most of an opportunity to discuss the story of past revivals and dreams and hopes of another in our generation.

The outstanding memory of my visit on Oxford's campus was the study-bedroom in Lincoln College where John Wesley and his young friends started the

"Holy Club" with its later development into the evangelical revival of the eighteenth century. Edwin and I felt constrained to pray there for a repetition of the movements of the eighteenth and nineteenth centuries. His word on revival caused me to do a great deal of thinking, which God used to bear fruit in later years.

Since 1949, in Minnesota, California, Washington and other states of the Union, Edwin Orr has been used mightily, particularly on university and college campuses. Great spiritual awakenings have followed in the wake of his ministry at Bethel College, Northern Baptist Seminary and other outstanding institutions. In late August 1949, it was my privilege to be one of the speakers at the Forest Home Briefing Conference, in the beautiful San Bernardino Mountains of California. The messages Dr. Orr gave as one of the other speakers were of tremendous blessing in my own life. His logical development of the whole subject of full surrender and the outpouring of the Spirit stirred the entire conference, evening by evening.

During the many intervening months we have remained in close contact. Dr. Orr's work among the stars and starlets of the entertainment world is already well known, and it was through that effort that I was led of God to make contacts which later resulted in the conversion of more than one Hollywood personality.

This present volume, Dr. Orr's fifteenth book, consists of chapters based upon those talks at Forest Home which provoked, under God, a real stirring among the students. I do not expect that all my Christian friends will agree with all the terminology used by the author of this book. I shall be disappointed if mere points of terminology are allowed to hide the spiritual arguments of the case which has influenced the thinking of so many. I write this introduction with the heartfelt prayer that the message of full surrender will produce much fruit in the lives of Christians who are hungry for spiritual quickening in these days.

December, 1950                          Billy Graham

# Publisher's Preface

In the Book of James, a powerful argument is made for the absolute necessity of a settled mind. In illustrative fashion, the half-brother of our Lord refers to a prayer for wisdom (1:5ff) and insists that if we ask for such a blessing we must do so in faith and without any doubting. The doubting asker is likened to the surf of the sea which is driven of the wind and tossed. Those who pray without having a settled mind on the subject are warned that they must not expect to receive anything from the Lord. Furthermore, James is led to plainly state that the double-minded man is unstable in all his ways. This position is clarified by references to both a brother in humble circumstances who is raised up and a rich man who is brought low, the implication being that when one prays he must be prepared to receive whatever the Lord sends, expected or unexpected, pleasant or otherwise. The prayer of wisdom can be changed to a prayer for reviving and the fullness of the Holy Spirit and the teaching is fully applicable.

Altogether too many persons have gained an interest here, only to lose it long before God met them in a fresh and powerful way. I am thinking now of a young man who told me that he had been praying for revival for more than a year, but that God had not answered and he did not know what to do. When asked if he would be praying for revival a year hence he made it clear that he was unclear on that subject.

With sadness I reminded him that one of the major differences between himself and God was that God knew whether or not he would be praying for revival a year down the road, and if God knew that he did not care enough about revival to keep praying for it he should feel no surprise or disappointment that God paid no attention to his prayer. I then urged him to study the first chapter of James.

Every believer who reads this book needs to arrive at a settled mind on this subject. To fail here is to miss much of what God has for you.

During the years it was my privilege to personally know J. Edwin Orr, I never knew a time when he did not have an enduring passion for both personal and corporate revival. As much as any man I ever knew, he believed in revival and in the Spirit's empowering. While he engaged in a multitude of activities, they all seemed calculated to enhance the prospect of God's doing in the twentieth century what He had done so magnificently in earlier generations. Yet, as he whimsically narrates in his epilogue, there was a time when he turned aside from his original calling, and during this period of double-mindedness was permitted by the Lord to serve Him with only a mere shadow of the power he knew in both his earlier and later life.

A major part of Dr. Orr's conviction concerning revival focused on the need of individual Christians to enter into the fullness of the life of Christ. From much study of the Word and from deep and lasting personal experiences he was convinced that no one could know God's all until God was in possession of his all. As Mr. Graham points out in his introduction to the first edition, this book was originally written as the result of glorious days of blessing among students in North America. In the years immediately prior to his death, Dr. Orr came increasingly to the conviction that grievous errors were gripping much of the church and these errors were both sapping the church of its vitality and hindering the prospect for another outpouring of the Holy Spirit in worldwide awakening. Because of this growing conviction he determined to bring out a revised edition of "Full Surrender" in the hopes that it would be a tool in the hands of the Holy Spirit in bringing the church and its wayward people to repentance.

Dr. Orr labored many hours over the revising and updating of the volume, making its message even more pointed and relevant for this crisis hour. In the providence of God, he was taken from this earthly scene before this revised edition made its way into public print. Before his death he had determined to give the book a new title. Knowing something of his dreams and aspirations for this volume, we have selected the title, "My All, His All," believing with the author that it is only when Christ has "Our All" that we begin to know "His All."

It is with great delight that International Awakening Press brings back into print this new edition of J. Edwin Orr's widely used book. We send it forth with the earnest prayer that it will accomplish far more than even he envisioned and hoped.

April, 1989 Richard Owen Roberts

# Chapter 1

## THE FIRST WORD OF THE GOSPEL

It goes without saying that a major concern of public health is what experts and laymen alike call "birth defects," the physical handicaps that afflict the unfortunates whose entrance into life was marred by some accident of nature, some deficiency of formation which cannot be blamed upon their progenitors.

Is it not also possible that many ills of the Christian life are due to handicapped beginnings in spiritual birth? That unfortunates, whose professed conversion was marred by a lack of understanding of what was involved, might find their spiritual life full of trials and woes not experienced by the children of God who were well born?

The news media made much of the announced conversion of a notorious pornographer whose journalism presented the public with smutty titillation which was not "naughty" but obscene. That he was "born again" on his own say-so was accepted by the press, but perceptive Christians waited for evidence of a change of heart and life-style. None was forthcoming. His first editorial after the event told the world that he now followed the spirit of Jesus and Buddha.

There must be millions of professed Christians, much less notorious, who have suffered a bad beginning in the Christian life, whose profession of faith was much less open to blunt questioning by thinking people. It behooves us, therefore, to consider the initial experience of the Christian life before we can consider the living of it. What exactly is involved in becoming a Christian? What does it mean to be "born again"? What does it mean to be converted?

It is interesting to notice the variety of responses when people are asked: "What is the first word of the Good News of Jesus Christ? Some say: "Only believe;" others say: "Love." Some say: "Hope;" others say "Heaven." And the odd person replies: "Liberty," or "Civil rights." It was one man's protest that "the Gospel is so rich in its meaning that it is not possible to state a first word: it has many words of significance."

The alphabet has twenty-six letters, each of them useful but some much more used than others. But ask any kid in kindergarten: "What is the first letter of the alphabet?" and he replies: "The letter A."

"And why is A the first letter of the alphabet?" And he says, "Because it is."

"But why do you say, 'because it is'?" And the answer comes back with its devastating logic: "Because it comes first in the alphabet."

Which then, among the many words of the Good News of Jesus Christ, is the first word? With which word does the Gospel begin? The preliminary approaches of the Evangelists (as the discussion of water with the woman at the well) need not distract us. What is the first word of the message of the Gospel?

If the first word in the mouth of John the Baptist was the first word in the mouth of the Lord Jesus, and if that was the first word in the mouth of the twelve disciples, and if that was the first word in the Lord's final instructions to His disciples, and if that was the first word of exhortation in the mouth of the Apostle Peter in his first great sermon at Pentecost, and if that was the first word in the mouth of the Apostle Paul throughout his ministry, surely that would be the first word!

So what was the first word in the mouth of John the Baptist? The third chapter of the Gospel of Matthew states it thus: "In those days came John the Baptist, preaching in the wilderness of Judea, 'Repent, for the kingdom of heaven is at hand.'" What was the first word in the message of our Lord? In the following chapter it is recorded: "From that time Jesus began to preach, saying: 'Repent, for the kingdom of heaven is at hand.'" Had the Lord Jesus preached before this? Apparently not. This then was His first message. And what was its first word? Unequivocally, it was the word *repent*. And the word occurs in verbal form three other times in the Gospel of Matthew, as part of the most compassionate of impassioned preaching of the Lord Jesus.

There are some who make a distinction between the Good News of the kingdom of heaven and the Good News of the kingdom of God. In the first chapter of the Gospel of Mark, it is recorded that after John the Baptist was put in prison Jesus Himself came into Galilee, preaching the Gospel of the kingdom of God, but the message was the same. After saying that "the time is fulfilled, the kingdom of God is at hand," the Lord said emphatically: Repent and believe in the Gospel. Also in Mark's Gospel, our Lord's calling and coaching of the twelve disciples is reported, after which "They went out and preached that men should repent."

Some may suggest that perhaps this first word *repent* gave way to some other exhortation as the ministry of the Lord and His disciples fully developed. The Good News according to Luke, after mentioning the initial use of the word *repentance*, records it another ten times in verbal or substantive form, always in the preaching of the Lord Jesus, whether impassioned or compassionate. What is most significant is that in the last discourse of Jesus with the disciples, as recorded in the last chapter of Luke's Gospel, He stated plainly that the whole purpose of His death and resurrection was "that repentance and remission of sins should be preached in His name to all nations," begin-ning from Jerusalem. This constituted as certainly the Great Commission as did the command of Matthew 28.

It is fitting to ask whether the apostles who received the final commission were faithful in carrying it out. When the Apostle Peter reached the climax of his first great sermon at Pentecost, and his hearers cried out in conviction: "Men and brethren, what shall we do?," Peter recalled the parting instructions of his Lord, and told them to "Repent, and be baptized every one of you for the forgiveness of your sins," which was exactly what he and his companions had been told to declare. In his second great sermon, Peter said the same thing in slightly different words: "Repent, and be converted that your sins may be blotted out . . ." That the Apostle Peter continued to preach repentance is clear from a dozen citations of the word in the Acts.

And did the Apostle Paul preach that same message? It is recorded that he was converted on the road to Damascus and began to preach, though the content of his message was not immediately recorded. But many years afterwards the Apostle himself declared what he had preached from the beginning: "I was not disobedient to the heavenly vision, but declared first to those at Damascus, then at Jerusalem, and throughout all the country of Judea, and also to the Gentiles, that they should repent, and turn to God, and perform deeds worthy of their repentance." The clear implication of the context is that he received a commission to preach repentance just as much as did the disciples in earlier times. And from other references in the Acts it is clear that he preached repentance to Jews and Gentiles.

Not only does the average Christian seem unaware of the first word of the Good News, but he apparently does not know at all what the word means. To the average man, the word *repent* means "to feel sorry." Show him an item from the newspaper that a murderer has shown no repentance whatsoever for his evil deed, and he will explain that "the fellow is not a bit sorry for what he has done."

The Greek scholar, Richard Trench, Archbishop of Dublin, defined the word repentance clearly as "That mighty change in mind, heart, and life, wrought by the Spirit of God." The word *repentance*, as used by modern Christians, does not signify a mighty change of mind, heart and life, but rather an emotional, sentimental experience better described by *regret* or *remorse,* for which an entirely different word is used in the Greek of the New Testament. The essential sense of the word *repent* is *to change.*

The Greek word *metanoia* is composed of two parts, *meta* meaning change, and *noia* meaning mind, hence *a revolution of thought.* But the meaning does not end there. It has a moral as well as an intellectual impact that is best summed up by the declaration of the Apostle Paul that he was commissioned to urge both Jews and Gentiles to revolutionize their thinking, and to turn to God and perform deeds worthy of their change of heart. Repentance may affect thinking, behaving, and feeling, as it was applied by Christ to Nicodemus, to the woman dragged by Pharisees before our Lord, or to the rich young ruler in early days; or as it now could be applied to a Buddhist priest, to an alcoholic, or to a lover of money on Wall Street. It clearly involved a thorough revolution of intellect, will, and emotion.

How then did the meaning of repentance shift from *a mighty change of heart* to a lesser sense of regret? It is because of the use of the Latin word *repentance* which was derived from *paenitentia*, or a sense of pain or suffering, hence the grief for an act which might demand satisfaction, or the sorrow looking back upon something amiss. Unfortunately, the word *repent* is also used in the English Bible for a Greek verb properly translated "regret." In the Prayer Book, the words *repentance* and *penitence* are used interchangeably, causing endless confusion to this day.

Some mistaken people voice the strange notion that the Apostle Peter preached a message of repentance to the Jews, while the Apostle Paul preached "only believe" to Gentiles, and that when the Apostle Peter first preached to the household of Cornelius he did not use the particular word *repent*. A cursory reading of the story suggests that this was so. Cornelius, a captain of the Italian regiment, was "a devout man who feared God with all his household, gave alms liberally to the people, and prayed constantly to God." He obviously was a God-fearer rather than a convert to Judaism. The account of Peter's ministry and the whole company's conversion contains no reference to repentance in word or deed. But the next chapter, which recounts how the Apostle explained to the church at Jerusalem his odd conduct in disregarding the rules of segregation, concludes that they glorified God, saying: "Then to the Gentiles also God has granted repentance unto life." Whatever Cornelius did, the Holy Spirit designated it "repentance." But wherein did Cornelius change, if change is the proper translation? Did he cease to be devout? Did he cease to fear God? Did he stop giving alms? Did he quit praying constantly? No! Wherein did he change? Up until he heard the message of Peter he was struggling to obtain salvation by his good works; but after the message, he put his trust in the finished work of Christ. That was a change of thinking indeed.

The word *repentance* or *repent* is used in the writings of Paul to the Romans, the Corinthians, and Timothy, and by the writer to the Hebrews as well as by the Apostle Peter. It even occurs ten times in the Revelation of John. In all of the New Testament it appears more than fifty times. Hebrews lists it as an elementary doctrine of Christ, a foundation stone. How serious then is the condition of a professing church when repentance is missing from elementary evangelism or church growth?

The three parables of our Lord in the fifteenth chapter of Luke's Gospel are often called "the Gospel Parables," or the parables of evangelism. They are the well-known stories of the lost sheep, the lost coin, and the lost son. The ending of each has a peculiar significance. The shepherd called together his friends and neighbors and invited them to rejoice with him that he had found his sheep that was lost. That is the end of the story, but the Lord quickly added: "Just so, I tell you, there will be more joy in heaven over one sinner who repents than over ninety-nine righteous persons who need no repentance." Why such an explanation? If he had not explained, someone would have insisted that as the sheep did not repent, there was not need of repentance for salvation. The woman who lost a coin called together her friends likewise that they might rejoice with her that she had found her lost coin. That is the end of the story, but the Lord quickly added: "Just so, I tell you, there is joy before the angels of God over one sinner who repents." Why the explanation? Some theologian might have insisted that as a coin is incapable of repenting, repentance is not needed for salvation. But the story of the lost son has no such explanation attached to its ending. Why? Repentance is clearly stated in the narrative when the prodigal son told his father: "Father, I have sinned against heaven, and in your sight; I am no longer worthy to be called your son." The addition, or lack of addition, of repentance is very significant, underlining its importance.

Sad to say, repentance is a missing note in much modern evangelism. The appeal is not for repentance but rather for enlistment. Thirty years ago, the notorious gangster, Mr. Mickey Cohen, attended a meeting in Beverly Hills which was addressed by Billy Graham and chaired by the writer. He expressed some interest in the message so several of us talked with him, including Dr. Graham. He made no commitment until some time later when another friend urged him, using Revelation 3:20 as a warrant, to invite Jesus Christ into his life. This he professed to do, but his life subsequently gave no evidence of repentance, "that mighty change of mind, heart and life." He rebuked our friend, telling him: "You did not tell me that I would have to give up my work," meaning his rackets; "You did not tell me that I would have to give up my friends," meaning his gangster associates. He had heard that so-and-so was a Christian football player, so-and-so a Christian cowboy, so-and-so a Christian actress, so-and-so a Christian senator, and he really thought that he could be a Christian gangster. Alas, there was not evidence of repentance. Many have sadly forgotten that the only evidence of the new birth is the new life. The real problem is that some evangelists, like some converts, have failed to recognize that the fault lies in the defective message.

Defective evangelism has become a national scandal. While evangelistic enterprises are claiming untold numbers of converts, a national poll announcing that multi-millions claim to be "born-again," yet a national newspaper notes that the "so-called evangelical awakening" seems to have had no effect upon the morals of the nation, while murder, robbery, rape, prostitution, pornography and the other social evils are abounding. The fault must lie in the message, for in the great awakenings of the past, sinners were urged to repent and believe the Gospel.

Many earnest Christians have raised the question: "Does not the Scripture teach that 'only believe' is all that is necessary? Did not the Apostle Paul tell the Philippian jailer simply: 'Believe on the Lord Jesus Christ and you will be saved?'" Quite so. But to whom were these words addressed? To a jailer who had cruelly beaten his helpless prisoners, but who was now so frightened that he had fallen on his knees to cry: "What must I do to be saved?" Had he repented? Of course. He had changed his attitude, so the Apostle reassured him that now all that he needed to do was to put his trust in the Lord Jesus Christ to be saved.

After all, there is no question that it was the Lord Jesus Christ Himself who said: "Repent and believe the Gospel." Some immediately react by supposing that this contradicts the "only believe" of the Christian message. Does "repent and believe the Gospel" imply that the sinner must do two things to be saved, and not one only? The exhortation is really only one requirement. The instruction: "Leave Los Angeles and go to London" may sound like two separate but related requests, but it really is only one, for it is quite impossible to go to London without leaving Los Angeles. It is likewise quite impossible to believe truly without really repenting. The difference between true faith and what the Scripture calls false faith is simple: it is the lack of true repentance. Without a doubt, many who seek to win sinners to the Saviour without specifying repentance in their Gospel presentation nevertheless hope that true repentance, that mighty change of mind, heart and life, will ensue, rejoicing when it happens. But their disappointment when it does not happen should compel them to reword their message so that there can be no misunderstanding whatever.

Strange to relate, many Christians do not realize that the word *repent* is also a word for the continuing Christian life. Not only is the word *repent* the entrance to new life in Christ, but it is an exhortation of Christ Himself for the believer in continuing in the Christian life. But that is a topic for consideration elsewhere. It is sufficient to emphasize in the present context that not only is evangelism defective without the opening word *repentance*, but that many baffled believers may be suffering defeat because of the primary neglect of repentance when they first professed to believe in the Lord Jesus Christ.

# Chapter 2

## THE FORGIVENESS OF SINS

---

It goes without saying that transgression of the laws of nature earns an inevitable penalty, as anyone who defies the law of gravity discovers at the bottom of a cliff. This is likewise true of the laws of health, for sleeping outdoors in mid-summer may be bracing, but in mid-winter definitely hazardous to health.

In a well-ordered family, a breach of discipline usually earns correction of some kind; otherwise family welfare is jeopardized. In a well-ordered school, insubordination is followed by a penalty. And disregard of traffic regulations earns a fine, or forfeit of time, to avoid chaos in the streets.

In every civilized society, a penalty that fits the crime is exacted for every breach of law. And in every military force a breach of regulations results in punishment, otherwise there would be no effective organization.

So it is not difficult to understand the logical basis for the principle taught in all the world's great religions: disregard of moral law entails punishment. Scripture clearly teaches the Christian truth that sin earns its wage, not by divine caprice but as a matter of consequence.

It is because of this that ethical religions are concerned with atonement and the forgiveness of sins. The Hindus have their law of karma. The Hebrews offered sacrifice. And the death of Christ, as an atonement, is central to the Christian faith and is clearly stated in its creeds: "I believe in the forgiveness of sins."

An inquiring cowboy in the Hollywood Christian group once asked me, "How does God forgive sins?"

"In Christ," I quoted, "we have redemption through His blood, the forgiveness of our sins . . ."

"You mean," he objected, "that Jesus died for me. I do not understand. How could anyone die for me? The Los Angeles police are holding a man for murder. If I go to the police and say, 'Let me take his place,' will they let me take his place? They will not. They will say, 'You did not commit the crime, so you will not take the punishment. It would not be right.' So, how could Christ die for me?"

"You have raised a difficult doctrinal issue," I replied. "Theological students study at least thirteen theories of the atonement, each one of which deals with a certain aspect. I do not think that I can explain the doctrine, but maybe I can illustrate." And I told him two stories.

Many years ago, when I was a boy of seven, I used to play ball "out the back" behind our house in the Ormeau suburb of Belfast. Diagonally across the lots from our home was the house of an unfortunate man, unfortunate only in the sense that his windows were always being broken by stray balls. He should have moved his house, we thought. One day, he came charging out of the house, waving an indignant fist: "The next one of you kids that breaks my window, I'll break your ear!"

We fled in distress. There was not much use in arguing with him for he possessed a one-track mind and would not listen to boyish reason. And who was the next one to break his window? I did not even stop to pick up the bat. The ball was doubtless under one of his beds, beyond recall. I ran instinctively for the shelter of home, but the news of my misadventure preceded me. My father was in the kitchen at the time and grabbed my wrist before I could make a quiet exit.

He insisted that I accompany him.

"I've brought you the boy that broke your window," he said. The man glared at me. Then he turned to my father and in a reasonable tone of voice said:

"Look here, Mr. Orr, I know that kids cannot help it, breaking windows. I used to break them when I was a boy myself. But it isn't right that every time a window gets broken around here, it has to be my window. I'm willing to forgive the kids, but somebody's got to pay for it!"

So, my father paid for it, and the man told me I was now forgiven, but not to do it again. And I carried away an impression in my mind concerning forgiveness: someone must pay for it. That was the first lesson.

Twenty years later, an Irish friend of mine borrowed a sum of money from me. He had been gambling and was in danger of losing his job. He agreed to pay me back in a hundred weekly installments, but he never did. I felt annoyed with the fellow for a couple of years. Finally, I decided to forgive him. But who suffered? The debtor or the creditor? The sinner or the sinned against? Obviously, the sinned against. I could have taken him to court, in which case he would have suffered. How much would he have suffered? The amount that he owed me! Instead, I forgave him, and so I suffered. I forfeited the amount that he owed me, that I had forgiven him. Thus I learned a second lesson in forgiveness: the one who forgives is the one who suffers.

I heard Bishop Stephen Neill once tell a hushed house of Oxford students that he had not fully understood the real meaning of the Cross until he heard an Indian Christian evangelist tell the story of the Prodigal Son in a market place in South India. The evangelist pointed out that when the prodigal had revolted against eating the husks fed to the swine, he was sorry for himself, but he scarcely understood the cost of forgiveness. Even as he walked his weary way home, reciting to himself the apology, "I have sinned against heaven and in thy sight," he could not have understood the enormity of his transgressions. And even when his father rushed out to meet him, even during the welcome-home banquet, he did not fully understand. It was not until some days later that the prodigal noticed that his father's hair had turned white in his absence. Then he understood.

Such reflection made the Cross much more real to me. It was necessary for someone to suffer, for someone had to pay. Because the one who forgives is the one who must suffer, it became necessary for Christ to suffer. Moses could not have suffered the Cross, nor Joshua, nor Peter, nor Paul, nor Mary the mother of Jesus. It had to be God, the only One who could forgive. God was in Christ, reconciling the world to Himself.

It is possible, therefore, to sum up the teaching of the forgiveness of sins of the unregenerate thus:

> The ground of forgiveness is the Cross.
> The price of forgiveness is nothing.
> The condition of forgiveness is conversion.
> The object of forgiveness is to obtain salvation.

No one who is familiar with the Scriptures will dispute the fact that the ground of forgiveness is the Cross, though there are many who overlook the fact. Nor will any insist that there is a price the unregenerate can pay: it cannot be bought, or earned or bargained for.

But there are some who confuse the forgiveness of sins unto salvation with the forgiveness of sins against keeping fellowship with God and one another. And there are some who may confuse repentance and conversion as a condition or requirement with conversion as a ground. No one is forgiven on the ground of his conversion, for there have been outstanding instances of non-Christian conversions to righteous living, such as Mahatma Gandhi. The ground of forgiveness is the finished work of Christ on the Cross, but it is also true that no one who has refused to repent and be converted has been saved.

But what about the forgiveness of sins of the believer? There is so much misunderstanding about this. A university student at Berkeley, a member of an evangelical church, once protested to me: "Why should I confess the cheating I did last week? I was converted ten years ago, and I am still a believer, so all my sins, past, present, and future are already forgiven."

When I asked her frankly if she were prepared to cheat in the next examinations, she hoped it would not be necessary!

The young lady was missing the distinction between the forgiveness of sins for salvation and the forgiveness of sins against fellowship with God and fellow Christians, a common misapprehension. Some good people refuse to use the Lord's pattern prayer because of the phrase: "Forgive us our trespasses as we forgive those who trespass against us." They protest that the sins of a sinner are forgiven not on that basis but freely, therefore the prayer is not for today. They forget that our Lord was talking to His own disciples, and that the prayer concerns fellowship with God and other consorts, not salvation. While the ground of forgiveness is the same, the Cross of Christ, God has promised to forgive the sins of those who are already converted on a different basis than conversion, otherwise all believers would need to become converted again and again, as often as they fell short of God's standards.

It was the privilege of the writer to direct a team of ten evangelists throughout a hundred campaigns in New Zealand and Australia in 1956 and 1957, among them the redoubtable Corrie ten Boom. One of the most spiritual women I ever met, Corrie had suffered severely at the hands of the Nazis in the 1940's. When she was finally released she left the concentration camp with bitterness in her heart against the whole nation of Germans. She found it difficult to forgive. Being devoted to God, she was contemplating missionary service, and was willing to go anywhere from Ahanghai to the Sahara, but not to Germany.

Darkness settled in her mind, and the petition in the Lord's Prayer frightened her: "Forgive us our trespasses as we forgive those who trespass against us!" She began to feel that if she could not forgive the Germans, God would not forgive her.

Knowing well that she had been brought up in a strong Calvinistic atmosphere, I asked her: "If you had continued to hold bitterness in your heart toward the Germans, and had gone to Indonesia as a missionary, would your soul's salvation have been in jeopardy?

"No, baas," Corrie replied. She had been brought up to believe in an eternal salvation, but she added that she was confused and depressed by the uncertainty. The cloud lifted when she asked God to help her to forgive.

I quietly showed her that the forgiveness of sins referred to in our Lord's Prayer concerned the failures of His own children who were already born again, and that they were sins against fellowship with God and others rather than sins requiring forgiveness for salvation.

This distinction must always be borne in mind. The real message for the believer concerning the forgiveness of the sins that mar fellowship is surely found in the words of the Apostle John in his First Epistle, chapter one:

> 5) This is the message we have heard from Him and proclaim to you, that God is light and in Him is no darkness at all.
> 6) If we say we have fellowship with Him while we walk in darkness, we lie and do not live according to the truth;
> 7) but if we walk in the light, as He is in the light, we have fellowship with one another, and the blood of Jesus His Son cleanses us from all sin.
> 8) If we say we have no sin, we deceive ourselves and the truth is not in us.
> 9) If we confess our sins, He is faithful and just, and will forgive our sins and cleanse us from all unrighteousness.

10) If we say that we have not sinned, we make Him a liar, and His Word is not in us.

There are some who mistakenly teach that the challenge of 1 John 1:9, "If we confess our sins, He is faithful and just and will forgive our sins and cleanse us from all unrighteousness," should be applied to the unbeliever or to the heretic. The epistle was written by a believer to other believers, and his declared object was the maintenance of fellowship between God and the believer. The key word is fellowship.

It is always important to recognize to whom an epistle is written. I have been asked to talk to teenagers upon "Love, Courtship and Marriage." If I were asked to address young married couples, I would certainly not speak to them as to unmarried teenagers nor advise them upon whom to marry. We must certainly keep in mind that the first epistle of John was written to those who are saved (who have been saved, who are being saved, who shall be saved), and it does not tell them how to be saved, but rather how to maintain fellowship with God.

The salutations of the Apostle underline the fact: "My little children . . ." "Beloved . . ." "See what love the Father has bestowed on us . . ." When the Apostle applied a truth to his readers, he used the pronoun "you." When he referred to apostates or unbelievers, he used "the one who . . ." Sixty times and more he used the pronoun "we," and in every case the context shows that he was including himself, as "any one of us." This makes invalid a claim by a very popular writer that verses 6, 8 and 10 in the first chapter refer to unregenerate people, whereas verses 7 and 9 describe the regenerate, even though the same "we" is used throughout. That writer even joins verses 4, 9, and 11 in the second chapter, verses which use "the one who" and obviously refer to unbelievers. The exegesis is clearly illogical.

From this passage it is seen that the forgiveness of sins against fellowship is also based upon the Cross, the blood of Jesus Christ, which not only cleanses us from sin in purchasing our salvation, but continues to cleanse us. (The Greek present continuous tense is used here.) So:

> The ground of forgiveness is the Cross.
> The price of forgiveness is nothing.
> The condition of forgiveness is confession.
> The object of forgiveness is to maintain fellowship.

No one is forgiven on the ground of his confession. The ground of forgiveness is the finished work of Christ on the Cross, but it is also true that no one who has refused to repent and make confession has enjoyed full fellowship. It is the testimony of many that when chastisement or revival has brought such unconfessed sins to judgment, fellowship has been fully restored, with joy unspeakable.

It is worth presenting a comparison of forgiveness for the unbeliever with forgiveness for the believer, for there are lessons to be learned:

> The ground of forgiveness for both is the Cross.
> The price of forgiveness for both is nothing.
> The condition of forgiveness is conversion (unbeliever).
> The condition of forgiveness is confession (believer).
> The object of forgiveness is salvation (unbeliever).
> The object of forgiveness is fellowship (believer).

Conversion is the key to salvation; confession is the key to fellowship. Conversion is the climax of evangelism, but not its end; confession is the climax of revival, not its end.

In comparing both forgivenesses, it will be seen that the ground is the same Cross of Christ, with a punctiliar application in the first instance and linear in the second. The price is the same to unbeliever and believer: it is not by works, for it cannot be bought, earned or bargained for, although works may follow.

The method of appropriation in both cases is the same, for forgiveness is accepted by faith. The forfeit is the same: Judgment, although in the first instance it refers to the Great White Throne, where eternal life is forfeited, and in the second to the Judgment Seat of Christ, where an account will be rendered by all the believers of deeds done, and where rewards are forfeited.

The crux of the matter for the Christian is obviously the question of confession of sins. Just as an unbeliever cannot negotiate his own forgiveness, but must repent and convert, so the believer cannot negotiate his own forgiveness, but must repent and confess. "If we confess our sins, He is faithful and just, and will forgive our sins and cleanse us from all unrighteousness" and "the blood of Jesus His Son cleanses us from all sin." Put negatively, if we do not confess our sins (against fellowship), God will then withhold the forgiveness and cleansing, and we shall remain without the blessing of full fellowship, like a disobedient child who does not cease to be a child though grieving his ever-caring parents.

Confession of sins is a neglected doctrine. It only comes into its rightful place in times of revival, when the Holy Spirit comes in doubly-convicting power and makes it impossible for the erring believer to have any peace of mind until the wrong is confessed whenever necessary.

# Chapter 3

## THE CONFESSION OF SINS

Christians sorely need a clearer understanding of what is entailed in the confession of sins. Recommended in both the Old and New Testaments and manifested in every spiritual awakening as the Spirit of God renews our feeble dedication, the confession of sins is beset by prejudice, ignorance, misunderstanding, and neglect in times of lessened zeal.

The word "confess" in various forms is utilized many times in the Old Testament, generally with reference to the open acknowledgement of sin. It is used more than a score of times in the New Testament with reference to confession of faith, but in several other instances to admitting sin.

What does the word really mean? When Simon Peter made his great affirmation, "You are the Christ, the son of the Living God," the Lord commended him, assuring him that the confession of his faith was revealed from heaven, and not by the opinions of men. He had expressed outwardly what the Spirit had revealed inwardly about the deity of Christ. Had he remained silent, would it truly have been confession? No! Confession of faith is something that needs to be openly expressed. It means much more than just "to agree."

Confession of sin seems to be the outward expression of what the Spirit of God has revealed inwardly. The Greek word rendered "confess" has two main components: "homo" meaning "the same," and "logos" meaning "word." We all tend to rationalize sin and disguise it; it is better to express agreement openly with the Spirit's verdict in our soul.

That "confession" means no more than "agreeing it was wrong," resulting in an automatic pardon, is suggested in a book by a very popular writer who, while "feasting on a bad thought," supposed that since he was "walking in the light as He is in the light" and having fellowship with Him, he was automatically cleansed from this and every other sin. Was Peter walking in the light and having fellowship with Him while thrice denying Christ as Lord? No! He was grieving Him, and when convicted, he wept bitterly and in sore repentance never denied Him again. There is no hint of repentance in this other story but only the remark, "Why make an effort to get out from under sin when Jesus says it's already gone?" which had a devastating effect on a young people's group in Covina which interpreted it to mean "its okay to shack-up for a weekend so long as you agree that it is wrong."

The Apostle John, who in his first epistle wrote, "If we confess our sin, He is faithful and just to forgive us our sin," also relayed the message of the Lord regarding confession of sins in the Letters to the Churches prefacing the Revelation. Therein the sins of believers were denounced, including lovelessness, lukewarmness, impurity, and pride. In every case, such wayward ones were ordered to repent. Yet I have heard of evil men recounting all their sins, bragging not confessing.

Seasons of revival generate denials that either public or private confession of sins is ever necessary, but too often the vehement protests have been prompted by unwillingness to right a wrong requiring an apology or restitution.

The Epistle of St. Clement shows that seasons of revival in second-century Corinth brought confession. Doubtless the confession and the sharing of their faults to ask for prayer and gain deliverance was practiced by the early churches. It is not our task to trace deterioration of confession until it ended in auricular confession to a priest, this based upon the mistranslation of a curious Greek tense for absolution.

In Protestant constituencies, complaints are often heard against confession made in public of vices better disclosed in private. In my own experience of over fifty years of real awakenings in many lands, I heard no breach of decency or of good taste where Scriptural teaching was given first.

Before the corresponding texts in Scripture are located, it is fitting to present a maxim of confession to put at ease the minds of those on edge: "Let the circle of the sin committed be the circle of the confession made." In other words, the sins secretly committed should be secretly confessed; private sins privately confessed; open sins openly confessed. The maxim is not meant to make an arbitrary prohibition.

## (1) Specific Confession.

Charles Grandison Finney wrote, "A revival of religion may be expected when Christians begin to confess their sins to one another. At other times, they confess in a general manner, as if they are only half in earnest. They may do it in eloquent language, but it does not mean anything. But when there is an ingenuous breaking down, and a pouring out of the heart in confession of sin, the floodgates will soon burst open, and salvation will flow over the place."

This has been demonstrated in every awakening or revival in the past two hundred and fifty years. This principle of specific confession is clearly taught in Leviticus 5:5 where it is said: "He shall confess that he has sinned in that thing."

During the 1952 movement of revival in Brazil, a lady in a crowded church confessed: "Please pray for me. I need to love people more." The leader told her gently: "That is not a confession, sister. Anyone could have said it." Later in the service, the good lady stood again, saying: "Please pray for me. What I should have said is that my tongue has caused a lot of trouble in this congregation." Her pastor whispered to the leader, "Now she is talking."

It costs nothing for a church member to admit: "I am not what I ought to be," or "I ought to be a better Christian." It does cost something to say: "I have been a trouble-maker in this congregation," or "I have had bitterness of heart towards certain leaders, to whom I apologize right now."

While attitudes to sin are general and may be recognized as such in general confession, all acts of sin are obviously particular and should be confessed in a particular way. A sinner overwhelmed by so many specific convictions of sin that he does not know where to begin, should start with his besetting sin, about which he feels the most conviction. The other sins may be confessed as guided by conviction.

### (2) Responsible Confession

Achan, a soldier in Israel's army, had disobeyed divine commands and military orders by looting gold and silver and expensive clothing; so, with God's blessing withdrawn, the armies of Israel tasted humiliating defeat at the hands of a tiny enemy garrison. Joshua told the looter: "My son, give glory to the Lord God of Israel and make confession to Him; and tell me what you have done."

Confession was first due to God against whom the sin had been committed, but it next became due to persons who had been affected by the sin, for the blessing of God had been withheld on account of one sinner. Achan was asked to make a confession of responsibility.

Before the 1949 college revivals in North America, I was preaching at a university in the Midwest. Encouraged by the noonday prayer meetings of the students on behalf of their unconverted fellows, I was dismayed that not one person we had prayed for had made a decision, although others personally contacted did so. The president of the local group was not attending many meetings because of preoccupation, his wife being in a nursing home with their first-born.

Then I was told privately that these otherwise admirable Christians had been married only five months. This bothered me less in spirit than the fact that six months previously he had accepted his election to the leadership, hypocritically. His open confession of a private sin appeared unnecessary, but for such unworthy conduct he should have offered his resignation. Some were prepared to renominate him, but fortunately, within the year, his organization asked him to resign, and then the students prayed for commenced to testify of conversions stemming from the meetings long since over.

### (3) Thorough Confession

Proverbs 28:13 is a clear call for thorough confession: "He who conceals his transgressions will not prosper, but he who confesses and forsakes them will obtain mercy."

Once a conviction of sin has been quenched, there is a tendency for the sinner to conceal or cover anything which remains as an unpleasant memory. The work of the Holy Spirit is to reveal such things. But it is the sinner's duty, with God's help, to forsake the sin confessed.

Two workmen in our engineering shop in Belfast came to blows and refused to speak to each other for several days. The other men ganged up on them and, protesting that the feud was hurting them all, urged them to apologize. This they did reluctantly, after which one told me, "If he ever says a thing like that again, I'll hit him on the nose again."

I heard of an Irishman in Mullingar who went to his priest and urgently requested a hearing of his confession. He then confessed that he had stolen two bags of potatoes. The priest, who knew the gossip of the town, suggested that it was only one sack of potatoes that had been stolen. Thereupon the man agreed that he had stolen only one, but that it had been so easy he proposed stealing the other one the next night.

Some confessions are not thorough. They are too

general, or are not made to the persons concerned; or they neglect entirely the necessary restitution; or they indicate no plans for a change of conduct in which the sin is really forsaken. In fact, they are only attempts at psychological relief. It is not enough to announce that one has cheated: a plan of restitution needs to be offered. It is not enough to admit having pilfered: the stolen goods must be taken back. It is not enough to confess that one has been malicious: the falsehoods or slanders ought to be confessed specifically.

### (4) Private Confession

Concerning private confession, confession made by one individual to another as distinct from secret or public confession, the words of our Lord, as found in Matthew 5:23-24, have clearest application: "So if you are offering your gift at the altar, and there remember that your brother has something against you, leave your gift there before the altar and go; first be reconciled to your brother, then come and offer your gift."

The offering in Hebrew sacrifice mentioned by the Lord was one accompanied by direct confession of sin to God for willful or inadvertent transgression. The Lord amended it to add confession to be made to persons hurt thereby.

Most Christians display a preference for confession in secret before God, even concerning matters which involve other people. To confess to God seems to them to be the easiest way out. Is it more important to be right with God or man? With God. With whom shall we put things right first? With man. God knows whether or not we have sinned; man does not know until we say so. If the offender were really conscious of the presence of God, even secret confession of private sin might lead to further action. Most offenders merely commune with themselves, for God refuses to listen under certain conditions.

Two people may agree to participate in sin. The offender convicted should confess his guilt to the other, denounce the deed, trusting his confession to awaken a sense of guilt in the other, then make right any wrong inflicted on others.

Confession of sins against sexual purity is more involved. In fornication, here defined as unchastity between an unmarried man and woman, the convicted person should renounce the sin to the other, making sure that the wickedness is never repeated. In adultery, here defined as unchastity between married persons not married to each other, the convicted person should urge the other to put the matter right with the other's wronged spouse, utmost discretion being needed in the marital relationship. It would certainly be unfair for a seducer to enjoy the pleasures of seduction and then glibly urge his victim to put things right with her husband. He should offer to share the blame and make things easier for his victim. In any case, an unfaithful husband or wife must consider the timing and circumstances of confession, and avoid unnecessary damage to the marriage, if it can still be mended by forgiveness sought earnestly and humbly.

A sinner may offend someone who is not a party to the act by consent. To use offensive language to a second person in the presence of a third requires an apology to both the second and third parties. The same thing applies to apology for loss of temper, confessing to all known witnesses.

### (5) Open Confession

"Therefore confess your sins to one another, and pray for one another, that you may be healed. The prayer of a righteous man has great power in its effects." This is the exhortation of James, the Lord's brother (5:16).

Although no limits to open confession are mentioned, they are implicit. What is the object of confession? Deliverance from faults. What is the means invoked? Prayer. How much then should be confessed? Just enough to enlist prayer. So unwise confessions seem to be as implicitly prohibited as insincere or vicious or profane confessions would be, and common sense tells us that just as descriptive details of a scheme of cheating without detection might bring temptation to others, so would confession of details of impure acts.

The pastor of a renowned New England church told me that an officer of his church, influenced by the practice of a popular movement, asked permission to make a statement to the congregation. It was both humble and sincere, but it concerned a sexual sin so distasteful that even the most spiritual hearers could not dissociate the memory of it from him in later days, though they all rejoiced that he had obtained deliverance from the vice. Almost all sexual transgressions are either secret or private and should be so confessed. A burden too great to bear may be shared with a pastor or doctor or a friend of the same sex. Scripture discourages even the naming of immorality among believers, and declares that it is a shame even to speak of things done in secret by the immoral.

Open confession was practiced during the baptizing by John the Baptist in Jordan, and following the preaching of Paul in Ephesus. It had limits, no doubt. The manifest concern for limiting open confession should not become an excuse for prohibiting open confession of a proper sort.

The peerless Greek scholar, Dr. A. T. Robertson, has observed that confession to God already is assumed in this exhortation of James, and that public confession of certain sins to one another in the meetings is greatly helpful in many ways. Though the King James Version uses the word "faults," the more ancient manuscripts and the more modern translations use "sins." The odd tense of the Greek verb "confess" here implies group confession rather than private confession between one individual and another, "ones to others," not "one to one other."

Group confession brings a psychological relief, but the motive should not be that. We make confession to gain spiritual healing, and the Greek word for healing given here is used elsewhere for the healing of the soul as well as of physical sickness. Group confession is not hurtful, for the individual is encouraged to forsake the sin and is helped by the knowledge that his sympathetic friends will pray for him, while others in the group are challenged to bring their own problems to the light. In times of revival, there are reports of a few unwise public confessions among an overwhelming number of restrained ones. The leaders have sometimes said that only fear of intruding into a work of grace had held back their advice or rebuke of indiscretion. It should have been given beforehand.

### (6) Cleansing Confession

The Apostle John declared simply: "If we confess our sins, He is faithful and just to forgive us our sins, and to cleanse us from all unrighteousness." Remembering that the promise is given to believers concerning fellowship rather than salvation, it offers not only forgiveness but a thorough cleansing of the life of the child of God. A driver may take his car to the garage because of a speck of dirt that blocks the carburetor; before the mechanics finish with it, he may get a thorough overhaul. So often the humble confessing of a fault has led to a thorough renewal of the whole Christian life, for the grace of God knows no limits.

# Chapter 4

## THE SETTLEMENT OF GRIEVANCES

The leading layman of a prosperous church where I once held meetings confidently told me: "What you just said about apologizing to someone I have wronged is something I have done for years. But if someone does me an injury, I wait until he comes to apologize to me. Am I right?"

I told him why I thought that he was wrong. The Lord Jesus prescribed His rules for reconciliation in simple terms: "If your brother sins against you, go and tell him his fault between you and him alone. If he listens to you, you have gained your brother. If he does not listen, take one or two others along with you, that every word may be confirmed by the evidence of two or three witnesses. If he refuses to listen to them, tell it to the church; and if he refuses to listen even to the church, let him be to you as an outsider and a tax collector."

The Lord's instructions further stated that whatsoever such a court should bind on earth must be that which shall have first been bound in heaven, and whatsoever they should loose, that which shall have first been loosed in heaven.

Who, in such a case, is innocent? I am, and not the other one. And who should then initiate a settlement? The guilty one? No, I should! But why? If I must make the move to right the wrong when I am found at fault, should not the guilty one then do the same? He should, but if he should ignore his duty, I must then respond. Why?

Any obvious breach between the brethren constitutes a wound in the body of Christ. Christians find it easier to walk in harmony with God than get along with one another. They irritate each other, hurt each other, quarrel with each other, and even take their feuds into the house of God.

I am reminded that on one occasion, we were entertaining guests within our home - a home of which I can affirm: "where seldom is heard a discouraging word, and the skies are not cloudy all day." The "donnybrook" erupted when one guest accused the other of failing to put on the potatoes while the rest of us attended church. The peace and harmony of home was rent asunder. They were eating our provisions, sleeping on our sheets, yet never thought to ask permission to stir up such a fracas to disturb the sabbath calm. So it is with God's own house, to which the brawlers bring their feuds. And so the innocent should seek for peace, for Jesus' sake.

But no! Offended folk, instead of seeking peace, enlist support and divide a church. Why did the Lord admonish "you and him alone"? Most Christians of goodwill embrace a chance to put things right, without humiliation. But there are some who falsify a conversation, or show irrationality. For them, a friend or two is needed to heal the breach, or otherwise as witnesses to prevent prevarication. And if he will not heed them either, the church should be informed.

The word translated "church" denotes "a gathering," and any gathering of saints to which they both belong will do: a choir, a Bible class, a congregation, an association. In such a body there is sense enough to settle things according to the Book. But both friends must welcome arbitration.

I learned of a case where two believers helped a third, investing funds while he provided talent. He dumped them later, slighting their financial partnership. A Christian panel tried to settle it on proper terms. He disregarded this, and finally was forced to take the verdict to a court of law.

Which issue raises questions: how should one treat a Christian who will not listen to the judgments of his friends and of the church? A tax collector must be treated with respect and honesty, but not with warm affection; outsiders should be treated with consideration and civility. Hence, a brother who refuses settlement should not be treated as a brother, should not enjoy our confidence. He should be given kind and civil deference and not be subjected to "the silent treatment," unless some immorality or stealing is involved, when all believers must not even eat with such a one.

But there are other complications. Suppose the witnesses or leaders of the church themselves are less than honest in their task and take the side of the unjust, what then? I have known of such a case, where leaders called to mediate a suit involving capital and property in millions announced in writing their intention not to judge the right or wrong or to take sides, but to concern themselves only with the control of future operations. They proceeded to harass the innocent, to cover up the guilty, and to try to seize control by ousting officers and board and even threatening to blacken the reputations of those who would not go along with them. The only thing to do was to defy their threats and go on cleaning up the operation.

In many instances, believers must remain content to let the matter go and leave its settlement until the judgment seat of Christ, when all believers answer for the deeds they did and forfeit possible rewards. But what if it involves a crime against the law, or money which was given for some stated purpose held in trust? Or where a slander forms a part of scheming to defraud? Resort to legal action may be unavoidable, but only as a last resort.

And what does the Scripture say of the magistrate? That believers should "do what is good and . . . receive his approval." But if they "do wrong . . . be afraid, for he does not bear the sword in vain; he is the servant of God to execute His wrath on the wrongdoer." The magistrate's authority has been "instituted by God," is God-appointed, and everyone, unbeliever or believer, obedient or otherwise, must "be subject to the governing authorities." Hence the magistrate is "God's servant for your good," wherever any breach of civil law occurs. (Romans 13:1-4)

Many Christian folk were taught that taking other saints to law is always wrong, and were quoted the Apostle Paul's counsel on "trivial cases" (I Corinthians 6:1-8):

> When one of you has a grievance against a brother, does he dare go to law before the unrighteous instead of the saints? Do you not know that the saints will judge the world? And if the world is to be judged by you, are you incompetent to try trivial cases? Do you not know that we are to judge angels? How much more, matters pertaining to this life! If then you have such cases, why do you lay them before those who are least esteemed by the church? I say this to your shame. Can it be that there is none among you wise enough to decide between members of the brotherhood, but brother goes to law against brother, and that before unbelievers? To have lawsuits at all with one another is defeat for you. Why not rather suffer wrong? Why not rather be defrauded?

It seems worth noting that the first of these seven verses is not the prohibition of taking another Christian to law, but rather taking him to law instead of taking him before a court of justice of the church. In fact, the verses focus on five questions, in each of which the burden lies upon the saints to solve disputes within the brotherhood. The last resort is to the law, and sometimes sad to say "unrighteous judges" show concern for righteousness that far exceeds regard for rights by many carnal Christians. God is a God of justice, and indifference to justice is offensive to His righteousness. Those who save themselves embarrassment by choosing not to be involved seem not to mind that others are defrauded, libeled, slandered, robbed and hurt.

For ourselves, we choose to suffer wrong or be defrauded in matters where we alone are hurt, but we never allow an officer in an organization handling the sacrificial gifts even of dying saints in terminal distress to misuse funds.

Some things the Christian brotherhood may not settle. If one among them is guilty of murder, neither the elders nor deacons nor the congregation can settle it. The most that they can do is to offer him spiritual help and urge him to surrender to the law. The same applies to embezzlement, in fact, to any criminal act. The law must take its course.

# Chapter 5

## THE SEARCHING OF HEART

The Holy Spirit is the author of revival, both individual and general. It is His ministry that brings a believer to a sense of need, that brings a congregation to repentance, that brings a whole community to transformation.

According to Christ Himself, the ministry of the Holy Spirit is to convince the world of sin, of righteousness, and of judgment; but many believers mistakenly rely upon their consciences alone rather than on a conscience that has been enlightened by the Word of God and quickened by the Spirit of the Lord.

The work of God's Holy Spirit, therefore, is to show the sinner just how far he has fallen short, to show him also the paragon of righteousness in Christ and to warn him of inevitable judgment. It is significant that the Holy Spirit carries out a corresponding work in Christians' hearts, convincing them of carnality, also a falling short, spurring them on to total commitment, which means appropriating the righteousness of Christ for every day of living, and also warning them of the judgment seat of Christ, where they may gain a prize or suffer loss.

It is to the Holy Spirit that the Christian must look if he ever is to find a measure of revival for his seeking soul. Certain blessing for believers is dependent on a cleansing, which in turn depends upon confession, that is dependent on conviction; and conviction comes with the searching of the heart by God's own Spirit.

The most effective prayer for a spiritually hungry believer is an eloquent petition found among the Psalms of David:

> Search me, O God, and know my heart;
> Try me, and know my thoughts;
> And see if there be a way of grief in me,
> And lead me in the everlasting way.

I never fully understood the profundity of this petition until I heard the verse translated into the Scandinavian tongues. There the word "search" is rendered "ransack." It takes not much imagination to picture the thoroughness of a job of ransacking, compared with a mere searching. Ransacking turns things upside down, and brings to light the things that are hidden or forgotten. In the usual times of backsliding, the Spirit of God is quenched and conscience smothered; and as life goes on, the natural tendency for a convicted person is to forget the unpleasant episodes. But in renewed conviction of sin, the debris of ordinary living is swept aside and the offending thing is brought again to one's attention. To avoid a superficiality in confession, a thorough ransacking of the heart by God is needed.

The petition is definitely personal: "Search me!" Far too often, the more spiritual members of a church or group are more aware of the glaring faults of their less spiritual fellow-members than they are of their own shortcomings. The proper emphasis is found in the negro spiritual song:

> Not my brother, nor my sister,
> But it's me, O Lord,
> Standing in the need of prayer.
> Not the pastor, nor the preacher,
> But it's me, O Lord,
> Standing in the need of prayer.
> Not the elder, nor the deacon,
> But it's me, O Lord,

Standing in the need of prayer.

The disciples did not say: "Is it Peter . . . is it James . . . or is it Judas?" but: "Lord, is it I?" There is a time for every purpose under heaven, and there is a time for healthy introspection. Our prayers go unheard until we cease to regard iniquity in our hearts, and only by probing the heart is the sin dragged out to the healing light.

It is significant that the petition is addressed to Deity. Neither pastor nor psychiatrist, physician nor psychologist, friend nor enemy, stranger nor familiar self, can adequately search the heart for sin. Sin offends Almighty God, and only God can bring to light its real offensiveness.

To their consultant, most inquirers will reveal only what suits themselves and spares their feelings. Be he ever so clever, a well-trained pastor or psychiatrist is limited by his prejudices, circumstances or training. All information brought forth for analysis is limited by the seeker's feelings, and the human judgment brought to the case is limited by the adviser's ideas. Man makes an inadequate analysis and a risky diagnosis. God makes no mistakes.

How often have I noticed with men in combat their proneness to tell me just enough to get me to agree with them, excuse the fault, and salve their consciences. Never did a soldier say, "It's much worse than I'm telling you," though usually that was the case.

Self is an even poorer judge of sin than some consultant. Man is utterly incapable of searching his own heart. Man will always rationalize his sin. I call to mind an old acquaintance in Illinois who appeared to be a pathological liar. He told his lies so often and so repeatedly that he soon came to believe them all himself. No one can be trusted to examine his own heart. The heart is deceitful.

Not only the heart but the thoughts need searching. There are some people who commit sin in the warmth of affection, or desire or passion. But others are cold-blooded in their contemplation of transgression. God searches both the heart and mind;

He tries the thoughts, for as a man thinks in his heart, so is he. Murder begins in hatred, stealing in covetousness, and adultery in impurity of thought. Imagination is often stronger than the will, and indulging it in the mind inevitably leads from thought to action.

The Spirit's searching of the heart and mind shows every believer how he has wandered from the way. Confession of the sin will lead him back to the path of fellowship. This in itself is spiritual revival, for the individual.

And is the Spirit's searching of the heart and mind wholly independent of close cooperation by the seeking Christian? By no means. A believer may fully cooperate with the Holy Spirit in such heart-searching. First, he must recognize his needy state and humbly acknowledge that his condition is not the will of God. Then he must pray and specifically ask the Spirit to search out his heart. Not only must he thus continue in prayer, in which the Spirit may convict him, but he must also give diligent attention to the reading of the Word, especially those injunctions suited to his need or his condition, for thereby also the Spirit will convict. And as well, he must insert the key to open up the vaults of memory and try to recall the acts or tendencies that have derailed his spiritual life. He may also seek the counsel of a friend, for sometimes the Holy Spirit puts His rebuke in the mouth of a faithful friend. He may even re-examine the unkind and unpleasant things said about him by his enemies and critics, who may be telling the truth, though saying it maliciously.

Lest anyone excuse himself because he is not conscious of the grosser sins, let him note that added to the prayer is a petition: "See if there is a way of grief in me!" Anything that grieves the Holy Spirit of God is a hindrance to His blessing, and stands in the way of revival.

And what is the way everlasting? Essentially, it is the Way - Christ Himself. "If we say we have fellowship with Him while we walk in darkness, we lie and do not live according to the truth." Walking in the way everlasting means walking in the light. It means walking in the truth. Christ is the Way, the Truth, and the Life. Walking in the Way and obeying all the Truth is the secret of abundant Life.

Of one thing a believer may be certain, that the Holy Spirit never leaves a seeking heart untouched. Skillful is all His surgery, tender all His healing. God's chastening is love.

# Chapter 6

## BROKEN VOWS

---

Why is it that hundreds of well-meaning Christians attend so many conferences and conventions for the deepening of the spiritual life, enjoy the ministry given there, return to life's vocations with a feeling of improvement, yet speedily relapse into their former ways of backsliding and defeat?

There are many reasons, but one of the least noted is the issue of incomplete consecration, the sin of broken vows. Too many Christians make a bargain with God and fail to pay their part of the price. A striking example is found in the story told by Luke in the Acts of the Apostles:

> But a man named Ananias with his wife Sapphira sold a piece of property, and with his wife's knowledge he kept back some of the proceeds, and brought only a part and laid it at the apostle's feet. But Peter said, "Ananias, why has Satan filled your heart to lie to the Holy Spirit and to keep back part of the proceeds of the land? While it remained unsold, did it not remain your own? And after it was sold, was it not at your disposal? How is it that you have contrived this deed in your heart? You have not lied to men but to God."
> When Ananias heard these words, he

fell down and died. A great fear came upon
all who heard it. The young men rose and
wrapped him up and carried him out and
buried him.

After an interval of about three hours,
his wife came in, not knowing what had
happened. And Peter said to her, "Tell me
whether you sold the land for so much." And
she said, "Yes, for so much." But Peter said
to her, "How is it that you have agreed
together to tempt the Spirit of the Lord?
Hark, the feet of those that have buried
your husband are at the door, and they will
carry you out." Immediately she fell down at
his feet and died. When the young men came
in they found her dead, and they carried her
out and buried her beside her husband. And
great fear came upon the whole church, and
upon all who heard of these things.

It is not my intention to dwell upon the judgment
aspect of the tragic story of Ananias and Sapphira.
Those days following Pentecost were days of revival,
and in such times the Holy Spirit operates in unusual
blessings toward the obedient and in unusual severity
toward the disobedient. In the narrative are lessons to
learned by all in all times.

It should first be noted that Ananias and Sapphira
had made a voluntary act of consecration. As the
Apostle Peter said, while the land remained unsold, it
was the owner's undisputed possession; and after it was
sold, the money realized thereby was the owner's
undisputed acquisition. No one told Ananias and
Sapphira that they must sell their property in order to
remain in Christian fellowship. No one compelled them
to offer the proceeds to the general fund of the infant
Christian Church. Their maximum inducement was the
power of godly example and exhortation. They had seen
others making a financial sacrifice, so they thought of
a way whereby they might gain like approval without
making the full sacrifice.

Likewise, the acts of consecration made by

Christians today are all voluntary. No one is told that he must spend so much time in prayer in order to remain in fellowship. Neither is any one told that he must give a tenth or more of his income in order to be recognized as a Christian. Nor is any one told that he must witness to so many people each week in order to prove that he is a true believer. All these things are done, but on account of godly example and exhortation rather than by compulsion.

Another noteworthy fact is that Ananias and Sapphira seemed unaware of the seriousness of their transgression. They appeared to be unaware of offending Almighty God at all. The Apostle Peter told the husband, "You have not lied to men, but to God." One cannot imagine that Ananias and Sapphira had sat together in conference and had planned to tell a lie to the Holy Spirit. The Holy Spirit was far, far from their thoughts. The Apostle asked them how they had schemed such a thing in their hearts, but it does not seem likely that either husband or wife fancied themselves in a battle of wits against the Holy Spirit. They were apparently totally unaware of His involvement.

So it is with Christians today. They scheme and plan and cheat and deceive in ways that involve the Holy Spirit, who cannot ignore broken vows. But the offenders are generally unaware of their sin. They think that it concerns themselves alone, and that failure is their own affair.

"How is it," asked the Apostle, "that you have agreed together to tempt the Spirit of the Lord?" It seems unlikely that they discussed the matter to the extent of saying, "Let us see how far we can provoke the Holy Spirit in this way!" The Holy Spirit was not in their thoughts.

And today many Christians, by keeping back part of the price of consecration, by making vows that are speedily broken, are guilty of provoking the Holy Spirit. No wonder they are making little or no progress in spiritual things. The fact that they have not suffered severely is evidence only of the longsuffering of God in times of spiritual decline.

In any case, Ananias and Sapphira suffered the extreme penalty as far as this life is concerned. There is dispute as to the future state of the erring church members. An ardent Philadelphian preacher has declared that Ananias and Sapphira were both genuine believers who offended the Holy Spirit and suffered a temporary judgment not affecting their souls eternal destiny. A zealous Chicago teacher affirmed that their hearts were filled by Satan and they went to perdition.

There is neither time nor space to explore these lines of argument. But there is agreement that the offenders had suffered an immediate breach of fellowship with God and His people, and that is what happens today to Christians who offend in the same way.

Fellowship, spiritual fellowship, is both vertical and horizontal, for "if we say that we have fellowship with Him while we walk in darkness, we lie and do not live according to the truth." The vertical fellowship with God is broken by cheating in consecration, by broken vows, and everyone who has fellowship with God has fellowship with children of God. When the vertical connection is broken, the horizontal lines are snapped as well, and fellowship, spiritual fellowship, between Christians is broken as the result of broken vows. But "fellowship" is a word which is used in a careless way by Christians. They seem to think that ordinary social fellowship between believers is truly fellowship in the spiritual sense because both parties are professedly spiritual. This is not so. Spiritual fellowship is the realization of the presence of the Holy Spirit between believers. When one or both or all parties concerned have grieved the Holy Spirit, there is no real spiritual fellowship. It is noteworthy that Christians offending the Holy Spirit sustain their fellowship on a carnal level, generally by criticizing maliciously the lives of other believers. They have no fellowship in love, but rather in common and carnal antipathies.

The penalty for trifling with the Holy Spirit is

breach of fellowship. For a while, the friends of the offender may not notice that he no longer walks with God. For a while, the offender himself may be utterly unaware of his breach of fellowship with God. The eyes accustom themselves to walking in the twilight of the sun that has set. But when judgment comes, the one who has trifled with God begins to realize that it is chilly after the sun has set, that he is walking alone, and that he is stumbling in the darkness. It is a lonely path for the backslider, who must surely ask: "Where is the blessedness I knew when first I sought the Lord? Where is the soul-refreshing view of Jesus and His Word?"

Had Ananias and Sapphira been better acquainted with their own Hebrew Scriptures, they would have found the warning of a very wise man against any trifling with Deity. The Preacher in Ecclesiastes gives a plain warning against making vows which are not meant to be kept:

> Watch your step when you go to the house of God; to draw near to listen is better than to offer the sacrifice of fools; for they do not realize that they are doing evil. Be not rash with your mouth, nor let your heart be hasty to utter a word before God, for God is in heaven, and you upon earth; therefore let your words be few . . .
>
> When you vow a vow to God, do not delay paying it; for He has no pleasure in fools. Pay what you vow. It is better that you should not vow than that you should vow and not pay. Let not your mouth lead you into sin, and do not say before the messenger that it was a mistake; why should God be angry at your voice, and destroy the work of your hands?

In 1939, I tried to enlist as an Air Force Chaplain, but it was late in 1942 before my services were accepted. In due course, I received an extract of orders "by Direction of the President" ordering me to active duty. I went and I went promptly! Sure, I had volunteered; but once my services were accepted, I neither argued nor delayed nor disobeyed. I respected military authority.

Shortly after returning to the United States from graduate studies in Oxford, I made a slight error of judgment and parked my car in a doubtful place in Chicago's Loop. Upon my return, I found a ticket tied to the windshield wiper, informing me that I had transgressed an obscure parking regulation and so was requested to appear at the Traffic Bureau on a day mentioned. I appeared. I neither argued, delayed, nor disobeyed. I respected the law.

The law has power to make me keep my obligations. How much more then should I respect the power of Almighty God? Too many Christians presume on the kindly fatherhood of God and forget that He is Lord of all. Therefore "watch your step when you go to God's house." The very thought of foolishness is sin, and it is foolish to trifle with vows.

"Be more ready to listen . . ." Too often prayer is a one-sided affair that degenerates into "Listen, Lord, Thy servant speaketh" instead of "Speak, Lord, Thy servant heareth!" God's calls are His enablings, so it is far better to listen to what God desires to tell us than to open our big mouths and promise what vanity and pride may prompt.

"Don't be rash . . . don't rush . . ." Weigh it up first. When my wife returned from Oxford's Radcliffe with our fourth child, I soon discovered that I was going to miss more sleep than in previous instances. My wife had a time table of feeding the infant: two, six, ten o'clock, every four hours. My wife knew the time table; so did her doctor; and so did the family; but apparently the new baby did not, nor did he seem to offer any alternative schedule.

So I found myself presented with two problems: one was how to get sufficient sleep, and the other was how to keep up my devotional schedule. A thought struck me one night. So I asked the Lord to let the baby sleep between his ten o'clock feeding and his six-in-the-morning one; and I also promised to get up at six o'clock for my quiet time. It was a wonderful idea. It seemed scarcely possible that it could happen. Alas, I did not tell my wife of my resolution, which showed my irresolution. I slept well, and the next waking moment was caused by the baby's whimper at three minutes before six. But I went back to bed. Three mornings in succession this happened. I found the warmth of bed too inviting compared to the chill of an English morning, and the fire died in my heart. From then on the baby boy continued in his own affectionate but wholly unpredictable way, and I missed more sleep than ever.

Under such circumstances, it is better not to vow anything to God than to vow and not pay. Sometimes Christians vow what is far beyond their capability, and they would do better to take a less ambitious stance. Some vows originate in pride, but God resists the proud and gives grace to the humble. It is better to say "The Lord enabling me, I shall do thus and so" and then to seek the necessary grace with a truly humble heart. The younger or less experienced the Christian, the more rash the vows.

"Let not your mouth lead you into sin." If a man's own tongue promises more than he fulfills, he thereby grieves the Holy Spirit. And the moment a man grieves the Spirit, he suffers a loss of sustaining grace, of which the Tempter is well aware. The wolf attacks the straggler, not the sheep that stays close by the shepherd. Broken vows bring about spiritual weakness, and spiritual weakness brings about temptation, and temptation sin. How little do believers realize the hazards of disregarding vows made to Almighty God Himself.

Too often, when a Christian makes a vow and fails to keep it, he explains it away as a mistake or as an error of judgment. Undoubtedly, there are instances when making a vow has been clearly a mistake,. but in most cases it has not been a mistake, and the undertaking vowed has been both worthy and possible. The error has consisted in the "falling short of the mark," another word for sin. When, however, a Christian has foolishly made a promise which he is incapable of fulfilling or which is unfortunate in its implications, the best thing to do is confess the lack wisdom in the vow to the Lord, to seek His release, and to ask for His gentle guidance as to the proper course to be taken. A vow should never be shrugged off.

"Why should God be angry at your voice, and destroy the work of your hands?" Not all prayer is acceptable, for the Scripture has declared that if one regards iniquity in one's heart, the Lord will not hear him. A broken vow is a sin of omission. It is also the commission of an affront to God. It must be confessed as sin before fellowship is completely restored. Otherwise, the discipline of God, the chastening of the Lord, begins to operate. It is necessary for the Lord to bring our schemes to nought in order that we may not stumble. Our friend becomes our opponent, not our enemy, and so says "check" to each move until, check-mated we begin again to walk more closely with Him.

Hence, in our searching of heart, it is imperative that the believer should cast his mind over previous times of sincere consecration, to check his record and see where he has failed to keep his word.

When a borrower goes to a bank, hoping to negotiate a much-needed loan, he should know that it is customary for the bank officer to look up his record in paying back previous loans. When a believer goes to the throne of grace, seeking blessing and making vows, he should know that he is appealing to One who remembers all previous occasions. God is graciously willing to help, but is waiting to hear the petitioner admit his failures honestly.

What then are the vows that Christians customarily make to Almighty God in times of blessing or on special occasions? More time in prayer, more intercession for others, more devotional reading, more study of the Word, more personal witness, more faithful tithing of talents and money, better example to others, patience with children, personal purity, self-denial.

These are the vows that are made in year-end watch-night services, prayer meetings, deeper life meetings, evangelistic campaigns, missionary meetings, and the like. How often these have gone unfulfilled.

Until broken vows are mended, it is difficult to make any progress along the way of consecration. Before seeking a blessing from God, one should carefully consider in honest retrospect one's previous dealings with Deity. It is not enough that no affront was intended. It is not enough that no deceit was planned in advance. The sin against Almighty God arises from a most serious transgression of the first commandment, that of nursing a coldness of heart toward the Lord Himself. Of that we must repent.

# Chapter 7

## SINS OF WRONGFUL POSSESSION

There is nothing more explicit in the Decalogue than the commandment, "Thou shalt not steal!" In the chaplaincy, I found that the commandment against stealing was the easiest to quote to show that the laws of God are not based upon the arbitrary whims of a Supreme Being unrelated to the good of the human race, which good is the will of God. It was so easy to picture the chaos which would result from wholesale departure from observance of the commandment against stealing. The test of mortality proposed by Immanuel Kant, its universality, was vividly illustrated for me when the palatial home of the notorious gangster, Mickey Cohen, a mile west of our family home, was looted by burglars one night, causing Cohen to remark: "What's the world coming to?" And I also recall the violent indignation displayed by a gang of Bengali train thieves robbed by a gang of Punjabis of the loot that they had taken from passengers.

### Stealing

In times of the moving of the Holy Spirit, professing Christians are often known to confess outright stealing. I have heard it said that it is superfluous to warn any Christian against stealing, seeing that Christians cannot steal and still be Christians! There is only one reply to that: both the

Apostle Paul and the Apostle Peter warned Christians against stealing, the former saying (Ephesians 4:28): "Let the thief no longer steal, but rather let him labor, doing honest work with his hands, so that he may be able to give to those in need," and the latter urging that no Christian should suffer as a thief (1 Peter 4:15).

There is only one thing to do in such a case: to make restitution; and if such restitution is beyond the power of the individual, he ought to throw himself upon the mercy of the person or persons from whom he

### Pilfering

Just as in the matter of lying, Christians find that their consciences are too tender for outright stealing, yet they often give way to some act they consider short of it. They pilfer little things; they misappropriate; they take what they consider unimportant things without permission. The Apostle Paul warns all Christian employees (or servants) not to pilfer, but to show complete fidelity (Titus 2:10).

It was said that during the Nicholson Awakening in the 1920s in Northern Ireland so many shipyard workers had come under conviction of the sin of pilfering tools and had begun to return them, that the management posted notices offering blanket forgiveness to all offenders but asked them to keep all such stolen tools at home because of the sudden overcrowding of the toolsheds!

A student attending college in the Pacific Northwest once approached me about the matter of pilfering, and when questions were asked, explained that he had "pilfered" a motorboat of considerable size! On the other hand, I have found Christians half-convicted about pilfering little things like postage stamps or telephone calls charged to the firm. Apply a simple test: if the employer agrees that privileges of the employee include free stamps and telephone calls, by all means take advantage of such generosity. Otherwise, it is petty pilfering, which is condemned in

Scripture.

Stealing is stealing, no matter how one may rationalize. In several revival campaigns, I have been approached by professing Christians who had become convicted about the pilfering of small sums of money from their employers, and, in each case, the excuse was the complaint that the employer had not been paying high enough wages. Alas for the excuse; the employer must be the judge of that, or, if he has actually cheated the employee of his just wages, the employee must appeal to the law, or union, not to private and surreptitious readjustment!

I have been asked hypothetical questions about stealing under circumstances of extreme necessity, such as some mountaineer with a broken leg, starving to death, dragging himself to a cabin which is well-stocked with food but with the owner away. I personally would have no compunction in such circumstances to put into operation immediately the principle involved in Deuteronomy 23:24, but offering to make good at the first opportunity. I suspect that the people so interested in such hypothetical emergencies are often more concerned with conscience-easing in the matter of other complicated misappropriation.

Scripture is explicit regarding sins of misappropriation by an employee: it is equally implicit about defrauding by an employer. The first six verses of James chapter five constitute as strong an indictment of such social injustice as any in literature. It is a sin for an employer not to pay a hired man a living wage (Malachi 3:5), to withhold his wages by fraud (James 5:4), to delay the payment of his wages (Deuteronomy 24:15), or to be inconsiderate of employees' complaints (Job 31:13). I wish I could say that such injustices were unknown among Christian employers in all ages, who have always shown their passion for social justice, but I certainly cannot. But social justice was the passion of six humble workers, known in trade-union history as the Tolpuddle Martyrs, who were shipped to the convict camps of Australia for forming a trade union to contest an employer's agreement to keep their wages at seven shillings (one dollar) a week. Five of them were local preachers or Christian workers, and the sixth was converted through their Christian witness in convict gangs.

Lord Shaftesbury, an aristocrat and a Christian, was Britain's greatest social reformer; and Keir Hardie, a coal miner but a reported convert of D.L. Moody, was Britain's greatest advocate of the rights of the working man, writing his first trade-union tract on Proverbs 30:8, "Can a man be a Christian on a pound a week?"

## Unpaid Debts

Stealing may manifest itself in the matter of unpaid debts. Every Christian is under obligation to pay back what he has borrowed, for it is a wicked thing to borrow and not to pay again (Psalms 37:21). Business investment should be distinguished from borrowing (in which the borrower has all the advantage), for an investor agrees to let a ready businessman use his money in an agreed, calculated risk. The Christian businessman will try to return both principal and interest to the investor, but there are circumstances where business failure should be borne and shared by all who had hoped to gain a profit from the business.

It appears from the Scriptures that debts are not to be repudiated or ignored (II Kings 4:7). The Apostle Paul has advised Christians to be in debt to no one (Romans 12:8). In view of the modern business practice of credit-buying, it should be pointed out that the sort of debt which Scripture condemns is neglect of meeting payment upon just contracts. Should a man lend a friend a sum of money for a year or so or until a certain date or circumstance in which the full repayment is expected, the debtor is not guilty of breaking his contract until the repayment falls due. In the western world it seems that most of the population purchase goods upon the installment plan. The purchaser therein makes a contract with the good will of the seller and providing he meets his installments promptly, he has not broken any contract. It is, of course, most unwise to purchase more than one's income can meet; but, even so, the purchaser may still ease his conscience by returning all the goods in good condition to the seller, who is generally and wisely safeguarded by insurance and by an appropriate down payment. Christians, whose day to day living is harassed by the demands of their creditors, would do well to sell out and start again.

Once I was lecturing in a London college when a burly Irishman stood up to demand: "D'you mean that a fella has to pay back the debts he contracted before his conversion?" Thinking of the principle involved in the case of Zacchaeus, I answered in the affirmative immediately. "Then," said he in disgust, "I'll be working from now until the millennium and then right through the thousand years!" Not wanting to rob the brother of the prospect of working a little for the Lord during that lengthy period, I inquired about the nature of the debts. They were gambling debts, he explained. He was reassured when I gave my opinion that such gambling debts were illegal and not binding. Anyone with any doubts about this should reflect that the first thing that a bookie does in order to collect one of his unenforceable claims is to try to persuade the debtor, often under threat of violence, to sign a chit for a legally enforceable contract to pay.

### Business Integrity

The Scriptures are also very clear concerning any sharp business practices against buyers by sellers, for "A false balance is an abomination to the Lord: but a just weight is his delight" (Proverbs 11:1). It is therefore very wrong for a Christian salesman to misrepresent the value of goods to a buyer. Proverbs 21:6 condemns the making of profits by misrepresentation and, according to Deuteronomy 15:13-16, it is unjust to have double standards in business. It is noteworthy that the "fixed price" was adopted by the Society of Friends as a result of the revival.

There remains the question of indebtedness to the

civic authorities, about which the Apostle Paul wrote to Roman Christians (13:6-7):

> For the same reason you also pay taxes, for the authorities are ministers of God, attending to this very thing. Pay all of them their dues, taxes to whom taxes are due, revenue to whom revenue is due, respect to whom respect is due, honor to whom honor is due.

Every great revival of true religion has sent conscience money to tax collectors from offenders convicted through the preaching of the Word or the operations of the Spirit.

It is certainly our conclusion that a Christian who has enjoyed the use or possession of another person's money or property unlawfully cannot enjoy the blessings of God at the same time. Property rights under law are ordained of God, and transgression of them is offensive to Him.

## Robbing God

There is a more direct affront to God, in the words of the prophet Malachi (3:8-10):

> Will a man rob God? Yet you have robbed Me. But you say, Wherein have we robbed You? In tithes and in offerings! You are cursed with a curse: for you have robbed Me, even this whole nation. Bring all the tithes into the storehouse, that there may be provision in My house, and prove Me now herewith, says the Lord of hosts, if I will not open you the windows of heaven, and pour you out a blessing, that there shall not be room enough to receive it.

To steal from a bank is bad enough; to steal from a benefactor is worse. Yet that is what so many believers do. By withholding their tithes and offerings, they rob God. Some avoid conviction by contending that tithing is only Old Testament Law, not binding on the Church today. One can only reply that if a Jew under the Law was obliged to give his tenth, a Christian under grace should do better than that.

The Apostle Paul insisted that just as those who were employed in temple service or who served at the altar received their sustenance through temple offerings, even so or in like manner, the Lord commanded that those who proclaim the Gospel should receive their livelihood though the Gospel (I Corinthians 9:13-14). The Christian ministry should be supported by tithes and offerings.

Some Christians say, at the end of the week (or month), "I do not have it to give." The Scripture teaches that we should lay aside our contribution at the beginning of the week. Too many believers are like the little girl who, given a penny for the Lord's work in the Sunday School and a penny for herself, tripped and fell, recovered one penny and put it in her pocket, but lost the other one down a drain, then exclaimed: "O Lord, there goes your penny!"

# Chapter 8

## SINS OF THE TONGUE

James, the brother of the Lord, devoted a chapter of his practical epistle to the subject of "control of the tongue." This chapter can be read without deep conviction, unless the Christian is willing to let the Holy Spirit search his heart for manifestations of the sins of the tongue, using the injunctions of Scripture as well as personal prayer, and facing the problem with honesty.

### Anger

While anger or bad temper, in an analytical sense, is a sin of the spirit, it so often results in the loss of the control of the tongue that it is here considered as a sin of the tongue. Anger has many varieties: indignation, resentment, passion, temper, wrath, ire, rage or fury; and these may express themselves in all sorts of ill-tempered words, ranging from the cold acid of sarcasm to the hot flame of fury. But every expression of anger is fraught with danger, not excepting even the most noble form of indignation.

It is very easy to remember that if one is in the right, they need not lose their temper; whereas, if one is in the wrong, they cannot afford to lose it. Angry words never improve any situation.

Hence, the Psalmist advised his friends (37:8) to cease from anger and to forsake wrath. And the world's wisest declared that a man slow to wrath demonstrates true understanding, whereas a quick-tempered man displays his own foolishness (Proverbs 14:29). Everyone knows that a soft answer turns away wrath, but grievous words stir up anger (15:1). A discreet man puts off his anger, but an angry one receives nothing but punishment (19:11,19). An angry woman is harder to put up with than life in the wilderness; while an angry man is so dangerous that one ought to avoid either a friendship or company with him (21:19, 22:24). Wrath is cruel and anger is out-rageous (27:4). So go the warnings of the writer of the Proverbs; so also Ecclesiastes (7:9).

Our Lord, in His Sermon on the Mount, declared that anyone who becomes angry with his brother is liable to judgement. The New Testament continued the emphasis of the Old on the subject of anger. The advice of the Apostle Paul, "Be angry but do not sin," is not a commandment to become angry, but prohibition against sinning in anger (Ephesians 4:26). In other words, the Apostle warned the Christians: "If you do let yourself get angry, be careful that you do not sin!" In the same letter, the Apostle told all his friends in the Ephesian church (4:31) to put away all bitterness and wrath, and anger and clamor, and he repeated the advice to the Colossians (3:8).

Christians excuse their bad temper in different ways, and some among the more carnal are actually somewhat proud of their uncontrolled spirit. I have heard a famous speaker describe from the pulpit how he lost his temper, and his account of these incidents showed not a trace of repentance, rather an ignorant pride. The more spiritual Christians, knowing that ill-temper is condemned, find a euphemism for their faults in describing them. One of the most common is to attribute bad temper to "nerves" and make an infirmity out of a fault.

It is far better to admit the fault, to repent and confess, to forsake it and to make a humble apology for it. God can give victory along the lines of greatest defeat. Bad temper under control becomes good temper, not an absence of temper. A person with a controlled temper can achieve much more than one without reserves of spirit.

## Profanity

In the third commandment, it is stated:

> Thou shalt not take the name of the Lord thy God in vain; for the Lord will not hold him guiltless that taketh His name in vain.

And the commandment was given by Christ:

> Do not swear at all, either by heaven, for it is the throne of God, or by the earth, for it is His footstool, or by Jerusalem, for it is the city of the great king. And do not swear by your head, for you cannot make one hair white or black. Let what you say be simply "Yes" or "No"; anything more than this comes from evil.

As a chaplain serving in the forces overseas, I can say quite simply that to me profanity was a sorer trial than any terror of war. Profanity included vulgarity, lewdness, sacrilege, and blasphemy, and the horrible mixtures of all four. By far, the worst was the taking in vain of the name of the Lord. The men used to tell me that they meant nothing by it, that they were not even thinking of God when they thus misused His name. More than once I told a flyer, "When your plane is hit by flak, and is tumbling fast to the earth below, you will scream God's name, and I hope that it will not be vain in its end result."

Why do men swear at all? Why do they use profanity so often? I found that men swore either to shock people, to be mean, or to hide an inferiority complex. Their profanity showed a lack of education, breeding and character. It lowered self-respect, cheapened the better things, and it defiled the whole personality. It shocked people of good taste, provoked contempt, and fouled the atmosphere. It set a bad example and disqualified men for decent society. From numerous references in both Old and New Testament Scriptures, it is clear that profanity always offends God.

Upon return to civilian life, I discovered that many men who were no longer moving in circles where foul language prevailed switched to minced oaths. Unfortunately, a large number of professing Christians quickly adopted the same silly and subtle vocabulary of simulated swear-words also. According to the Webster Unabridged Dictionary, such silly words as "gosh" or "gee" are minced oaths, euphemisms for "God" or "Jesus." A minced oath is recognizable by similarity to consonants or vowels occurring. in the original oath. Everyone should recognize "darn" as a substitute for "damn," and "heck" as a substitute for "hell," and other words as substitutes for expressions too crude to be even hinted at in print. Expletives beginning with a letter "g" or "j" or "c" should always be suspect. Expressions commencing with the preposition "by" are nearly always substitute swear words even if their point is blunted by the use of the name of some derelict god or other nonsense.

For any Christian to excuse his substitute oaths by saying that he means nothing by them, and is not even thinking of the real significance of the words, sounds exactly like the feeble excuse of profane swearers everywhere. It jars a tender memory to hear professing Christians, including leaders, use words which had an ugly origin in vulgarity or lewdness, even nice old ladies using expressions which in their original form would shock users speechless. The best way to avoid using language which sounds profane to the initiate is to avoid using all extravagant expletives. The obedient Christian wants to avoid the very semblance of evil. Experience has proved that a new convert can eliminate oaths from his vocabulary; likewise a spiritual man can eliminate minced oaths.

Let the person who is inclined to scoff at a condemnation of fashionable expletives remember that Christ Himself taught that unnecessarily garnished language is a product of evil. The Lord's brother James taught that the man who can control his tongue can control his whole personality; so let the scoffer try to eliminate his questionable epithets for a month. If he cannot do it, he is in bondage to a bad habit; if he can do it, he will find that the habit is utterly unnecessary. Only verbal cripples need crutch words.

> Let no evil talk come out of your mouths, but only such as is good for edifying, as fits the occasion, that it may impart grace to those who hear. And do not grieve the Holy Spirit . . .

## Lying

I doubt if anything is more clearly condemned in the Holy Scriptures than lying. Christ characterizes the Devil as a liar thus (John 8:44):

> When he lies, he speaks according to his own nature, for he is a liar and the father of lies.

Thus the Genesis story attributed the fall of man to the lying and deceit of the Serpent, and Revelation predicts that all liars shall have their lot in the lake of fire, the second death. The Ten Commandments condemn any false witness, and the Lord God told Moses and the Children of Israel directly "neither lie to one another" (Leviticus 19:11). The Apostle Paul has echoed the same words: "Do not lie to another" (Colossians 3:9), and: "Therefore, putting away false-hood, let every one speak the truth with his neighbor" as stated in Ephesians 4:25.

The Psalms condemn lying, and so also do the Proverbs. The Prophets warn against it, and so also do the Apostles. The references to lying in the Bible are too numerous for comment. Obviously lying is a serious sin.

Among worldly people lying is not regarded as wickedness. Without a blush people tell each other about the lies that they have told for their own advantage. Providing no other point of self-esteem is outraged, the hearer is not offended by the bragging about the cleverness of deceit. No one remarks, "But that was untrue!" with simple disdain.

On the other hand, only the most carnal of Christians will unblushingly admit lying. Christian conscience is outraged by downright lying. Most Christians will make an effort not to tell a lie. But if the circumstances prove embarrassing, many will not hesitate to lie their way out of a difficulty and consider it to be the lesser of two evils, the other evil apparently in their opinion being the consequences of their telling the truth.

Stricter Christians, however, will avoid lying and despise and distrust those who practice the vice. Some of the more spiritual Christians find their temptation in equivocation, or exaggeration, or understatement, or the similar giving of wrong impressions. All these shortcomings of the truth are refined lying. Charles Grandison Finney, who applied a fine mind and legal training to his evangelism, wrote his opinion pungently:

> Understand now what lying is. Any species of designed deception. If the deception be not designed, it is not lying. But if you design to make an impression contrary to the naked truth, you lie. Put down all those cases you can recollect. Do not call them by any soft name. God calls them Lies, and charges you with Lying, and you had better charge yourself correctly. How innumerable are the falsehoods perpetrated every day in business, and in social intercourse, by words, and looks, and actions designed to make an impression on others, for selfish reasons, that is contrary to the truth.

Lying, in my thinking, is any calculated form of deceit. It is possible to tell what is the truth and yet to convey a false impression. For example, an American evangelist came to visit me at Oxford University, which was many thousand miles away from his home.

Anyone in Oxford could have seen him running around the place with a pretty blonde. Were I not to add immediately that his wife was the blonde concerned, I would be guilty of lying. Suppression of pertinent parts of the truth can become lying. Telling what is not proven true does not necessarily constitute lying. At the moment of writing, I would be quite ready to inform any inquirer that my brother is living in London; yet a long distance telephone call might prove me very wrong for the moment, but so long as I said what I believed was true, I would be innocent of lying. But in certain circumstances, to discover that one had made a statement that was not proven true requires correction of a wrong impression.

Lying lips are an abomination to the Lord; their worst form appears to be lying with regard to spiritual matters, for it was Satan who filled the heart of Ananias to lie to the Holy Spirit. That he did not realize it was not an excuse.

## Criticism

The word "criticism" is defined in the dictionary as "the act of criticizing, especially in disparagement" or as "the art of judging with knowledge and propriety." The latter is a virtue and the former is a vice and one with which I propose to deal, for it is none other than the apostolically condemned sin of malice, for which Christians use the much softer word, criticism.

There is a great deal of difference between constructive criticism and destructive criticism. A loving wife will criticize her husband without any unloving thoughts arising. A loving parent will criticize his child without cessation of affection. A loving brother will criticize in the same way, always with the purpose of helping and not hurting. But the root of unkind criticism is selfishness, a selfishness which thrives on depreciating others, therefore wholly negative.

Many years ago, in New Zealand, I received a letter from a Christian minister in Canada, apologizing for having criticized me so unkindly that he had actually persuaded people not to go and hear me preach in the Massey Hall in Toronto. There were four pages of sincere apology, and only the last few lines gave me any clue concerning the nature of the criticism he made. In those days, being only twenty-three years of age, I had grown a mustache to hide my obvious immaturity. The Toronto brother felt that a fellow sporting a mustache like that could not be living very close to the Lord! Although I wrote a letter of tactful forgiveness immediately, I chuckled for days over the petty nature of the criticism. Then it suddenly dawned upon my mind that the real reason for his critical attitude was not the mustache, however much it outraged his sense of propriety: it was his lack of love for a brother in Christian service. I never forgot the lesson.

Surely lack of love for the brother is the root of all the unhappy criticism and divisions in the Christian fellowship. We neither practice nor permit malicious criticism of those who are dear to us, including ourselves. We rather criticize our own shortcomings in Christian love. We forget that God loved us when we were yet so very unloving.

With regards to criticism which intends to be helpful, the friendly critic should ask himself several questions before passing on a criticism to the one criticized. First: "Am I just as willing for an equally severe examination of my own conduct?" Second: "Is my motive in making this criticism sincere love for the person concerned and concern for the Lord's name?" Third: "Is the criticism calculated to correct the fault or merely relieve my own irritation?" Failing to pass these tests is more likely to hurt than help. Likewise, when some Christian feels it is his duty or has been asked to give his opinion of the conduct of another Christian, he should test his motives, not only with these first and second questions foregoing, but another: "Would I be willing to make the criticism to the person criticized?" or: "Have I tried to rectify the fault of my brother?" The words of the Lord Jesus Christ are perfectly clear:

> Judge not, that you be not judged. For with the judgement you pronounce you will be judged, and the measure you give will be the measure you get. Why do you see the speck that is in your brother's eye, but do not notice the log that is in your own eye? Or how can you say to your brother, "Let me take the speck out of your eye," when there is the log in your own eye? You hypocrite, first take the log out of your own, and then you will see clearly to take the speck out of your brother's eye.

It was Robert Doing, the Anglican lay evangelist in New Zealand and Australia, who reminded us that far too many Christians excuse their criticism of another's "speck in the eye" by disclaiming any "log" in their own, admitting perhaps a little speck of fault only; whereas, the "log" in their own eye is not a molehill of a fault but a mountain of resentment against the other person.

The Lord's advice does not mean that any of us should be tolerant of evil, but rather that we should always deal with the wrongdoing in our living first The Apostle Paul warned the Corinthian Christians not to associate with anyone who called himself a Christian but disgraced the name, and he added in 1 Corinthians 5:12: "Is it not those inside the church whom you are to judge?"

The same Apostle (Ephesians 4:31) urges believers not only to put away all malice, but he specifies slander; and in the law, actual slander need not be something utterly false, but a true statement maliciously uttered just to hurt another's reputation. In the letter to the Colossians (3:8) malice and slander are mentioned again in condemnation.

In the matter of confessing and making amends for an unkind criticism, a person convicted needs tact as well as frankness. If a Christian has made a hurtful statement about another Christian to a third party, the third party should also be informed that the statement made was false or malicious. The second person, the offended one, may not have even heard the criticism, and so it is not always necessary to confess the details of the criticism to him, for fear of unnecessarily wounding his feelings; only the spirit of criticism should be confessed in this instance.

Likewise in making open confession of a spirit of criticism, care should be taken not to give a wider currency to the malicious statement. It behooves every convicted Christian to pray for wisdom in making restitution of wrongs.

### Levity

In Ephesians 5:4, the Apostle Paul warns against levity, which is defined as unseemly frivolity or jocularity, as well as silly talk, and which, in the Greek original, suggests "talking like a moron." A. T. Robertson distinguished between "nimbleness of repartee" on the one hand and "ribaldry" on the other. The distinction in the Greek is worth making in the English, for there is all the difference in the world between a humorous frame of mind and a propensity for foolish jesting.

Bishop Taylor Smith used to pray in his English way: "Grant unto us, O Lord, the saving grace of a sense of humor!" A humorous disposition is a saving grace, for it comes from a correct sense of perspective. People with that kindly sense are never arrogant or proud or spiteful. They more often than not depreciate themselves rather than others. They try not to hurt, and they are willing to tell a joke against themselves. Their gift should never be equated with wise-cracking. A humorous disposition provides the salt that helps us masticate the tough fare of life. It cheers up others in their troubles. Jesting, on the other hand, is not fitting. It often makes its jokes or thrusts at the expense of others. It is generally vulgar. It is the enemy of serious conversation. It achieves nothing. It should be avoided no matter what the example may be. Humorous remarks may help at a

Christian banquet or youth rally; jesting often hurts, and sets the meeting back.

## Grumbling

Nearly every church endures a grumbler, to whom nothing seems right. He grumbles at everything under the sun, and he is the despair of all his friends. Grumbling is also a sin of the tongue, a habit pattern which betrays a spiritual condition. A Christian who is full of love, joy, and peace does not grumble, even though he may be enduring heavy trials. The grumbler is in rebellion, not only against petty circumstances, but against God. The Apostle Paul exhorted the Philippian congregation (2:14) to "do all things without grumbling or questioning!" The very first dispute in the Christian Church came about through grumbling (Acts 6:1), and the bad business has been going ever since. The best cure for grumbling is prayer and praise, which go in pairs, "for he has praises who has prayers."

## Foul Talk

Impure conversation is the deadly enemy of spirituality. Foul talk is condemned in the Ephesian letter (4:29 and 5:3-4, 12); but as the subject is part of the larger topic of impurity of thought, word and deed, it will be treated in another section.

# Chapter 9

## SINS OF IMPURITY

In the Scriptures, no other sin is mentioned more often with disapproval and threats of punishment than unchastity, carnal vice in its various forms, for no other sin is more impulsive and widespread than sexual sin. There appears to be no other area of human life in which unrighteousness has wreaked more havoc than in sexual relations. How many lies have been told to cover up? How many murders have been committed, how many crimes of passion? The sorrow caused by murder is of short duration compared with heartaches brought about by adultery.

Among Christians, the discussion of impurity is deemed distasteful. If unchastity reared its ugly head only among unbelievers, this Victorian taboo would make some sense, but what pastor, teacher, evangelist or chaplain would deny that sexual impurity is a major threat to the believer in his Christian life? Between the Victorian conspiracy of silence on the subject and a modern racket of talkativeness, the Christian has a middle course laid out already for him, to teach the precepts of revealed truth in the language and emphasis and balance of Scripture itself.

There is much that is different about the sin of sexual license. A man may lie, but he may apologize. A man may steal, but he may make restitution. But the licentious man is often guilty of damage that cannot be undone, resulting in the ruin of a character, the havoc of a home, the hurting of a family, the harming of a church.

Undoubtedly, the 1960's brought a flood of immorality upon society at large. In times of war or revolution, the Enemy of the Faith usually takes advantage of the turmoil to attack God and morality. Alongside noblest enterprises on behalf of civil rights, there were adolescent uprisings to secure all-night visiting privileges for both sexes in dormitories provided for by taxpayers' money. The permissive society began its almost irreversible corruption of young people, as relations between the sexes were no longer considered the foundation of family life, but rather a form of popular and private entertainment.

It seems that standards maintained by Christians in any given society lie halfway between those of the Scriptures and those of that society. The desperate poverty of some third-world societies has shaped the habits of the people so much that at post office counters there are signs: "Ask the postal clerk to postmark your letters in your presence," otherwise all stamps of value might be taken off the letters. Christians there scarcely stoop so low, but in many of the churches, there are two to count the offerings and one to watch them do it. In the same way, in the West, the given standards of the Christian youth lie halfway between the Scriptures and those of the entertainment world.

At a well-known Christian college, a young lady told me: "My boyfriend says that there is nothing in Scripture to forbid premarital sex relationship."

"You can't be serious," I replied.

"I could not think of any verse," she said.

"I'll quote you one," I answered. "Flee fornication" and then I added from another version: "Every other sin which a man commits is outside the body; but the immoral man sins against his own body. Do you not know that your body is a temple of the Holy Spirit within you, which you have from God?" (1 Corinthians 6:18).

"But what has that to do with premarital sex?" she said.

"Fornication," I explained, "is the English translation of the Greek word for premarital sex relationship."

"My boyfriend says," she told me the next day, "that was said by Paul, a woman-hater. But Jesus said: 'Neither do I condemn you.'"

"Neither do I condemn you," I quoted, continuing, "Go and sin no more!" But you want a verse which reports the words of Jesus regarding premarital sex relationship? It is not what goes into a man that defiles a man, but what comes out of his heart. And out of the heart come evil thoughts, murders, fornication . . ." (Matthew 15:19).

"All right," she said, "but why would it mention such an innocent thing as premarital sex along with murder?"

"They both begin in evil thoughts," I told her. "Murder is depriving one of life, destroying life; but fornication is a trifling with the power God gave us to create life, for we are joint-heirs of the grace of life."

In his advice to Christians, the main idea in the mind of Paul appears to be that fornication breaks the spiritual bond between the Christian's body and Christ, and makes the body itself the instrument of sin in a way not true of other sins. Such immorality is capable of blighting the body with a loathsome disease, and, worse again, of cursing an unborn child in the same way, hence it is a deadly vice.

The problem for young people is that this is the tender passion. A thief is not possessed by tender thoughts when robbing an old lady of her purse. A killer is not possessed by tenderness in murder. But for young unmarried couples the temptation to premarital indulgence is camouflaged by tender feelings that normally enhance the act of love for a couple fully committed for a lifetime marriage.

"But if a guy and a girl love each other," protested one young fellow, "what's wrong with it?"

What's wrong with it? If a fellow, taking his

pregnant girlfriend to a concert, skids his car into a
truck, killing himself, even though he has left a
fortune in insurance, the girl or unborn child has no
legal claim to it. This is social irresponsibility of the
worst kind. How can a man who says he loves a girl so
jeopardize her happiness?

Because of such temptation, the Christian who is
anxious to maintain his consecration must pay attention
to a threefold line of security: thought, word, and
deed.

## Thought

During antediluvian days of deterioration, "God
saw that the wickedness of man was great upon the
earth, and that every imagination of the thoughts of
his heart was only evil continually." Human nature has
not changed, for, "as a man thinketh in his heart, so
is he" today. In the words of Christ (Mark 7:21-22):
"Out of the heart of man come evil thoughts . . . fornication . . . adultery . . . licentiousness . . . an evil
eye . . ." Most temptations to impurity in the imagination are of a visual nature for menfolks. It was so
with Samson, with King David, and with righteous Job
who found it necessary to say (Job 31:1): "I made a
covenant with mine eyes; why then should I think upon
a maid?" As the Lord Jesus said (Matthew 5:28): "Every
one who looks at a woman lustfully has already
committed adultery with her in his heart." The Apostle
Peter denounced those (II Peter 2:14) who had "eyes
full of adultery, insatiable for sin."

The Christian should protect his eyes. He should
avoid any company which is provocative. Most of all,
he should guard his mind in times of relaxation,
remembering that it is always dangerous to give way to
thoughts of sexual indulgence when impossible or
inconvenient for legitimate fulfillment in marriage. The
unmarried should always avoid mental indulgence, and
the married should avoid a thought of even legitimate
indulgence when such occurs in the absence of the
married partner, for in the first instance there may
come a temptation to fornication and in the second

instance to adultery, in the modern sense of those terms.

Purity of thought is the defender's first line of resistance for the Christian. One who is pure in thought is so seldom caught unaware by temptation to impurity of action. "Each person is tempted when he is lured and enticed by his own desire. Then desire when it has conceived gives birth to sin; and sin when it is full-grown brings forth death" (James 2:14-15).

## Word

Most Christians instinctively shrink from impurity of conversation also. Thoughts with which they flirt in the hidden chambers of the mind are not permitted to expose themselves to the critical ear of other Christians. Yet, in practice, many Christians have intimate friends with whom they lower the barriers to improper conversation and lewd jesting. They maintain a double standard, and they become embarrassed when quoted outside their intimate circles.

"Let no evil talk come out of your mouths," wrote the Apostle Paul (Ephesians 4:29; 5:4); and "Let there be no filthiness." Sex should be treated as a sacred subject, and never as a sport.

It is wise for the Christian also to avoid discussing the scandals of the wicked, for the very discussion of them may conjure up defiling mental images. It is a shame even to speak of the things they do in secret (Ephesians 5:12). Many a chaplain would give a lot to be able to forget what he was forced to hear.

Christian girls would do well to avoid discussion of sex matters with eligible young men; there is a loss of modesty involved. In the godless world, seducers brag about their progress from mundane conversation to dangerous subjects. Even with men who have no thought of seduction, too frank a sex discussion with an eligible girl becomes temptation. One would not recommend the frank discussion of marital matters with even a lover until the wedding day has been fixed, and the discussion should then be a common-sense planning of married life, not a mental anticipation of the pleasures forbidden until the union is sanctified by the marriage of the couple.

In modern educational procedures, a certain amount of co-educational discussion of sex in scientific terms seems inevitable. The Christian student will let such discussions end in the classroom, so far as they concern the opposite sex. It is permissible to condemn by Scriptural word or godly counsel all impurity presented in conversation. Now, in the permissive society, the innocent believer should be alert to the efforts of conniving teachers to exploit attitudes revealed by means of scheming questionnaires.

### Deed

It goes without saying that the inevitable outcome of undisciplined thinking is undisciplined action. Among the adolescent, and also among those who never grow up, the practice of solitary impurity is widespread.

The modern fashion is to excuse such bad habits as mere immaturities. Hence non-Christian psychiatrists seek to relieve the feeling of guilt from the weakling. Comparisons are made with the lower animals, statistics are quoted, but they do not make right what is wrong.

The procreative apparatus in man was designed by the Creator for use in prescribed circumstances, sanctified by marriage. All other use is therefore abuse, and is so often followed by more serious sins. The cruelty of a sex-crazed sadistic killer may be traced back through perversion, then through fornication, then through secret vices to impure thought. Impure thinking may not go so far, but no one who gives way to it can tell how far it may lead him into vice.

The Psalmist prayed to be delivered from "secret faults" and "secret sins." It takes the light of God to deliver such sinners from "what they do in the dark, every man in the chambers of his imagery" (Ezekiel 8:12).

The word "fornication" is mentioned in condemnation in a dozen books of the Bible, but it is less often mentioned in Christian preaching and teaching, chiefly because it is so distasteful. In the Scriptures, the word is used in at least three ways: figuratively, to describe idolatry which sin is regarded as unfaithfulness to God and intercourse with wickedness; generally, to describe all sexual immorality, modern translators using the last-named word; but also particularly, to describe illicit sexual intercourse on the part of unmarried couples, even casual couples, which is the modern usage as defined in the dictionary.

The Scripture is explicit. The Apostle Paul advised the Corinthians (1 Corinthians 7:1-2) that it is good in principle for a man to have no physical contact with women. But because of the temptation to casual immorality, each man should have his own wife and each woman her own husband. What applied to the permissive society of the first century may be applied as thoroughly to the permissive society of present times.

The Scriptures make no allowance for unmarried people to indulge in sexual intercourse for any reason or for any excuse. The average Christian seems aware of the utter impropriety of casual relationships. But most Christian young people face their temptation in steady courtship, and they are sometimes willing to consider an increasing intimacy as permissible on account of their genuine love and honest intentions. This is a snare to them. "If they cannot exercise self-control, they should marry. For is it better to marry than to be aflame with passion" (1 Corinthians 7:9).

The answer to the problem of the strain of courtship is marriage, the proper state for the exercise of genuine love. There is no answer to the problem of either casual liaison or prostitution, except to abstain utterly. Such fornication is wickedness. Every Christian ought to know this, and yet one knows of so-called Christians who think that illicit sex liaisons are permissible so long as the precautions against pregnancies are taken. The first Corinthian letter (5:11) teaches clearly that Christians are not to associate, not even to sit at table, with an admitted fornicator who claims that he is a Christian.

"Adultery" is defined in most dictionaries as voluntary sexual intercourse by a married man with another than his wife, or by a married woman with another than her husband. In Old Testament Scriptures, "adultery" is used to specify sexual intercourse by a man, married or unmarried, with the wife of another man. Adultery in both the dictionary and in Scripture signifies a breach of the integrity of the family unit established by God as a sacred institution in society.

That the testimony of the Scriptures is unanimous is very certain: the seventh Commandment categorically prohibited adultery, and the law prescribed the death penalty for both adulterer and adulteress. Job characterized it as a heinous crime (Job 31:11). The Old Testament prophets always condemned adultery, and the New Testament writers also expressed their condemnation.

In civilized societies, while marriage customs vary much in detail, there is a uniform condemnation of adultery. No political party advocates adultery even though its members may practice such a vice openly or privately.

Problems of adultery should not arise for any Christian couple. Both husband and wife should see to it that their mutual love is well established and maintained in every way: spiritual, mental and physical. Alas, it is a deplorable fact that far too many marriages of Christian couples are not completely mutual. There is something wrong if the sacred relationship in its physical aspects should mean pleasure for one and anything less for the other. Sad to say, the ignorance of some Christians on the subject is appalling, while solution to the problem is so simple.

Since the 1960's, the western world has been faced with the problem of homosexuality in a way unknown since the triumph of nominal Christianity over paganism. Until the homosexual sub-cultures began to form political pressure groups to seize the balance of power in key cities, there seemed to be general agreement that homosexuality is an aberration. Since then, it has been proclaimed as one of two alternative life-styles, but no evidence has been ever submitted that it is a natural way of life.

The sexual apparatus in mankind, male and female, is a marvel of ingenuity. Were it not so delicate a subject, its ingenuity could be cited in detail as an argument, second to none, for design by a beneficent Creator. Heterosexual intercourse makes common sense; homosexual intercourse makes utter nonsense.

Physically considered, homosexual conduct produces a rate of venereal disease six times greater than that of the misconduct of heterosexual people in prostitution or casual liaison. Spiritually, it is generally utterly unsatisfying, and its emotional turmoil produces higher rates of murder.

What does the Scripture say: "For this reason, God gave them up to dishonorable passions. Their women exchanged natural relations for unnatural, and the men likewise . . ." Despite the rise of homosexual "churches" catering to the unnatural relationship, the testimony of Scripture remains: "Do not be deceived; neither the immoral, nor idolaters, nor adulterers, nor homosexuals . . . will inherit the kingdom of God." There is hope of salvation for all such sinners in the sequel: "And such were some of you. But you were washed . . . you were justified . . ." (1 Corinthians 6:9-10).

# Chapter 10

## SINS OF THE SPIRIT

Most Christians are startled when they learn that the sins of the spirit are a far greater hindrance to spiritual revival than the sins of the flesh. This contrast can be seen in the attitude of our Lord who was doubly lenient with the woman taken in adultery, and trebly severe with the pride of the Pharisee. This does not mean that adultery is less culpable than pride, but rather that one who gives way to pride is harder to help than one who gives way to adultery.

Our Lord spoke forcefully of the Pharisee who prayed "with himself" and thanked God that he was not like other men, extortioners, unjust, adulterers, or even like "this tax collector," boasting that he fasted twice a week and tithed all that he received. The tax collector stood back in his abasement, beating his breast and saying only: "God be merciful to me a sinner." He returned to his home "set right" rather than the other. The Lord's commendation did not mean that it was immaterial to fast and tithe and unimportant to refrain from extortion and adultery, but that the pride expressed in his words was sinful.

### Pride

"God resists the proud, but gives grace to the humble" (I Peter 5:5). The first sin of Satan, the angelic being created perfect, was pride, which was the iniquity found in him. (Compare Ezekiel 28:15ff and Isaiah 14:12ff.) His ego, inflated with sacrilegious pride, asserted itself in a five-fold defiance of God: "I will ... I will . . . I will . . . I will . . . I will . . . !" His sacrilege was summed up in his boast: "I will make myself like the Most High."

The heart of pride is egotism, or self-centeredness. The self-centered man is really eccentric, coming into collision with everything moving. The humble man is God-centered, and so finds his orbit in proper relationship with the orbits of all other men who are also God-centered.

Pride is too high an esteem of oneself for one's talents, or achievements, or merits or position. The humble man is not unaware of privilege of talents, achievements, merits or position, but ascribes them to God and submits them to God's purpose for his life and the cause of Christ.

Vanity may be an empty or mistaken pride in imagined attainments or an inordinate desire for the notice, approval, or praise of others. The humble Christian is not without a desire for notice, approval, or praise, but he seeks first the notice, approval and praise of God, and abhors the praise of men when it is in conflict with the approbation or evaluation of God.

Conceit is vanity added to pride. It is so supercilious that it thrives upon the depreciation of others. A conceited man tends to be forever trying to put others down.

There is another type of pride, inverted pride, more common in England than in North America, in which one takes pride in not appearing to be proud. Such cultivated self-depreciation, if undertaken to gain the approval of others, is just as deplorable as bragging. It is hypocritical humility. The story is told of the Oxford Grouper who had raised his self-evaluation in honesty, purity, and love to A, but struggled hard to improve his grade in humility; and when at last he succeeded, wrote a booklet on "Humility, and How I Achieved It." Humility is not achieved, it is the absence of pride or its reduction to simple self-respect.

## Hypocrisy

Hypocrisy is a spiritual sin for which Christ reserved His strongest condemnation. He had very little patience with the Pharisees, telling them (Matthew 23:28), "So you also outwardly appear righteous to men, but within you are full of hypocrisy and iniquity." Hypocrisy is nothing more than pretending, playing a part which is not in keeping with the truth. The Pharisees were concerned with the minor details of the legal code but neglected the weightier matters such as justice, and mercy, and faith. It was not that they were condemned for their over-strictness, but for their sad neglect of concern for other's rights. Any Christian who strikes a spiritual pose and does not live up to it is an obvious hypocrite.

## Neglect of Prayer

Prayerlessness is another sin of omission. It is a sort of creeping paralysis, which begins in neglect of prayer and ends in utter prayerlessness. Prayerlessness is a root of sin. By a neglect of prayer, a Christian becomes prey to a hundred vices. All sorts of creeping things crawl underneath the heavy stone of neglect, which once removed causes them to scurry away from the sunshine of fellowship with God. By neglecting prayer, a Christian robs himself of the counsel of God, quenches the Spirit, and hinders his growth in Christ. He finds it easier in prayerlessness to harden his heart against his brother, friend, and associate. The only cure for prayerlessness is prayer. Such prayer should begin with a confession of the sin of prayerlessness. If the prayerless one still finds it hard to pray, then he should start to praise the Lord for His many wonderful benefits. If praise does not loosen his tongue, he should then confess the sin of ingratitude.

In confessing any prayerlessness, the Christian should remember that lack of intercession for others to whom it is promised is also sin. The prophet Samuel stated: "God forbid that I should sin against the Lord in ceasing to pray for you." A Christian should be especially careful about keeping his promises of regular intercession made to missionaries, whose service is so sacrificial.

It is quite impossible for one Christian to arrange a programmed order of devotion for another Christian. It is even impossible for a Christian to prescribe one for himself. Prayer is unprogrammed devotion to God. Just as some affectionate husband does not tell himself, "I must set aside a dozen minutes daily for kindly words with my wife!" so a Christian cannot allot his time to the Lord. The loving husband gives all the time that he can to his wife; and the faithful Christian turns his thoughts to God each time that they are not necessarily preoccupied with something else. As the lyrics in the negro spiritual song express it: "Every time I feel the Spirit moving in my heart, I will pray!"

The best plan for prayer is that of the Psalmist, who prayed every "evening, morning, and at noon," or morning, noon, and night. Bedtime is not the best time for prayer, for we need it least in the land of nod. The best times are before undertaking the responsibilities of the morning, the afternoon, and the evening. This is not to say that a "good night" prayer is out of order. But, along with regular recourse to prayer, the believer should be ready to turn to God every time a decision is to be made, a contact to be exploited for Christ, a temptation to be resisted; in fact, every possible moment which can be devoted to contact with God should be given to prayer.

### Neglect of Reading

Devotional reading is likewise neglected by far too many Christians. It is often more important to begin by reading the Word than to pray first. It is more important that the Holy Spirit should have the opportunity of speaking to us through the Word than that we should unburden ourselves of our habitual utterances. The Lord can surely care for us without our telling Him, but we cannot obey His voice without hearing it.

Neglect of family reading is a common temptation of all Christians. Modern life is so crowded that opportunities for corporate family worship are few. Yet family prayers make a great integrative force. The Christian family which prays together, generally stays together; and the Christian couple who pray together seldom contemplate divorce.

It does not take much reflection to see that devotional reading, like prayer, done from a sense of duty only, is profitless. No doubt there is something to be said for encouragement to set aside regular times for devotions, but not in any mechanical fashion. The Christian who times himself may find that the very timing of devotion is despiritualizing.

Likewise, Bible study should not be made to do duty for devotional reading. Any reading of the Scripture necessary for the proper preparation of a sermon or lecture or talk should be treated as part of that service, and not allowed to crowd out devotional reading needed for the nourishment of one's own soul. The reading of doctrinal matters, in which one has a hobby interest, should be avoided during the quiet time, as should study assignments.

What should a Christian do regarding the many plans presented for reading the Bible through in a year? It all depends upon the time available during the waking day. If such a plan results in skimming through, so that little or nothing is learned thereby, then the project should be given more time. And certain parts of Scripture, such as the genealogies, are better suited to special study than other parts which seem more immediately profitable for teaching and training in righteousness, for reproof and correction.

## Neglect of Witness

Neglect of witness, which is better called cowardice or indifference, is another besetting sin of spiritual people. They render lip-assent to the need of witness, but seldom do anything about it; they rescue the perishing occasionally in the stirring stanzas of hopeful hymns, but they do not put their sentiments into practice in real life outside the church building. So Christians find it easier to talk about the weather, business, family, politics, sport, or almost anything but Christ. Are they ashamed of Him?

As with prayer and reading, witness should not be made a kind of bondage. I remember well a friend who was moved to learn that D. L. Moody made it a practice to speak to at least one soul each day about salvation. My friend adopted it with enthusiasm and it became a blessing to him, until he valued more his project than the soul he sought to win.

## Lovelessness

Lovelessness seems to be the cause of neglect of prayer, devotional reading and of soul winning. Lovelessness is the greatest sin of all, for Christ Himself declared that the first and greatest commandment is: "You shall love the Lord your God with all your heart, and with all your soul, and with all your mind, and with all your strength" (Mark 12:30; Matthew 22:36). So transgression of the first and greatest commandment constitutes the first and greatest sin. Lack of love for God breeds lack of love for fellow-man, for the second great commandment is declared to be: "You shall love your neighbor as yourself." Some Christians' love grows cold because they cannot accept the all-lovingkindness of God, that everything which He permits to happen to His child is allowed in love, for God is love.

## Unbelief

Unbelief is the final sin. Any Christian may repent of his pride, hypocrisy, prayerlessness, neglect of reading or of witness, and lovelessness, but if he is unbelieving and hard in heart, the Lord can do nothing for him. Thus Jesus was unable to do many mighty works because of the unbelief of His fellow citizens in Galilee. The writer of the Epistle to the Hebrews (3:12) names unbelief as the beginning of backsliding in the warning: "Take care, brethren, lest there be in any of you an evil, unbelieving heart, leading you to fall away from the living God."

Our salvation comes by faith. By faith comes also every subsequent blessing, whether of repentance, or confession, or forgiveness, or cleansing, or victory, or commitment, or filling, or call, or service. It is by faith that we walk, and unbelief is departure from the walk of faith. Whether it exists as petty worry, or occasional doubt, or continued unbelief, it is not of faith, and whatever is not of faith is sin (Romans 14:23).

What the Scripture reveals about God is true, hence it is impossible to exaggerate the importance of believing in the Word. Feelings follow faith, faith is placed in facts, and the facts are well presented in the Scripture. A study of the promises of God provide the antidote for unbelief.

# Chapter 11

## THE CLEANSING OF THE CHRISTIAN

In the inquiry room of an evangelistic campaign recently, I overheard a zealous Christian worker tell an unconverted man that all his sins could be forgiven and cleansed if he would only confess them. The worker assured him that the Scripture said so, in 1 John 1:9: "If we confess our sins, He is faithful and just and will forgive our sins and cleanse us from all unrighteousness."

This seems to be a common misapplication of a familiar promise made to believers. No one can promise cleaning through confession to an unregenerate man. No one has the right to tell a gangster that if he takes a full-page advertisement in the city newspapers to confess his sins against society, he will automatically receive cleansing from God. God requires the unconverted man to repent and become converted and receive the Lord Jesus Christ as his Saviour.

The word "cleansing" (katharsis) in its various forms is translated as "clean, cleanse, prune, purge, purify," in the New Testament, meaning either physical, medical, legal, ceremonial, or spiritual cleansing.

In fact, the subjects of spiritual cleansing are always believers in Christ, and the doctrine of "katharsis" is a doctrine of the purification of saints, not of the justification of sinners. It is true, however, that the repentant sinner, upon acceptance of Christ, is justified, and then enjoys the initial cleansing of the blood of Christ, by the Word of God. But no unjustified man is cleansed.

Christ's conversation with Peter (John 12:3-11) showed that the disciples had been laved (cleansed wholly) by the Word, but still needed a washing of the feet. The cleansing of the Blood of Christ is continually effective; but initial cleansing and periodic cleansing both are for Christians.

There is a difference between forgiveness and cleansing. Hitherto, I had always regarded the promises of 1 John 1:9 that "He will forgive us our sins and cleanse us from all unrighteousness," as a double biblical way of describing the same blessing, but I have come to see that two different things are promised therein. The things that are forgiven are acts of sin, specific sins; the thing that is cleansed is the whole personality, cleansed from all unrighteousness.

Our youngest boy was told many years ago not to play in a tempting mud-puddle. He disobeyed. To his dismay, he discovered that the muddy evidence of his disobedience was written all over his face, hands, knees, and clothes. Fearing a promised punishment, he stayed out late, until the twin forces of fear of the dark and miserable hunger drove him home. By this time, we were so relieved to see him that we forgave him promptly; but as soon as he was forgiven, his mother took him to the bathroom and stripped off his dirty clothes, washed his dirty face and hands and knees, thence into the tub for a complete bath, finally giving him a shampoo. So he went to bed, not only forgiven of his disobedience, but clean as a new pin.

A friend of mine left his car in the garage to be checked out for a speck of dirt in the carburetor. The mechanic discovered that not only was the carburetor dirty but that the car required new spark-plugs, new distributor points, new radiator hose, new rear tires, and a wax-job. So what began as a minor adjustment ended in a thorough overhaul.

I cannot forget the testimony of a young lady at Bethel College in Minnesota soon after the student body had been moved to seek forgiveness. "I want to thank God" she said simply, "for loving me enough to want to clean me up after all this mess I have been in." That has been typical of the many college revivals known to me. The misery of painful confession and reconciliation has always been followed by a period of cleansing so convincing to the students that the campus has been swept by infectious praise. The joy of the Lord was unmistakable.

It is not enough to preach the Word until Christians are convicted, have confessed, and are forgiven. They must be urged to accept by faith the promise of a general cleansing of the whole personality which happily God performs once a humbling occurs regarding a specific sin. Such times of revival are remembered as much for their joy as for their cleansing.

In the Old Testament, there is a story which illustrates the difference between forgiveness and cleansing. Psalm 51 was written by David after he, a man of God, had sinned grievously. Nathan the prophet had told the King that he was the guilty one, and David readily admitted his guilt, saying, "I have sinned against the Lord!" Thereupon, Nathan assured David the Lord had put away his sin. His sin was forgiven.

Did David believe the promise of God in the assurance of Nathan? Did he still cry out for forgiveness of adultery and murder? Psalm 51 was written soon after the day that Nathan had rebuked David for his sin. In its heart-felt petitions, there is no request for forgiveness, but many for cleansing. David had caught a glimpse of the uncleanness of his inmost heart: hence his prayers were for the blotting out of his many transgressions, the washing thoroughly from all his iniquities, the cleansing from his sin. In his Psalm, he asked the Lord to purge him as with a broom, to wash him whiter than snow.

"Create in me a clean heart, O God, and renew a right spirit within me!" That was not a prayer for forgiveness, for David had been told that his sin had been forgiven when he repented and had confessed. It was a prayer for complete cleansing.

In the New Testament, the Christian is told that if he confesses his sins, God is faithful and just to forgive him his sins, and to cleanse him from all unrighteousness. No, this wording is not accidental. Many a time, a Christian has become deeply convicted of some particular sin, and has at last confessed it, seeking forgiveness; but with the forgiveness of the particular sin has come a realization for a need of cleansing from inward sin, cleansing from all unrighteousness. The cleansing covers a larger area than that of the original area of conviction.

During the striking revival at Nigaruawahia in the Waikato in New Zealand in 1936 (described in an article by Oswald Sanders entitled, "We were as Men that Dreamed" and published in the periodical of the Bible Institute of New Zealand), I was moved to write the words of a prayer-hymn which was set to the tune of an old Maori folk-song "Po Ata Rau" ("Now is the Hour"). The prayer-hymn was published that year and has since been going around the world. Its words reflect the biblical teachings:

> Search me, O God, and know my heart today,
>     Try me, O Saviour, know my thoughts, I pray;
> See if there be some wicked way in me,
>     Cleanse me from every sin and set me free.
>
> I pray Thee, Lord, to cleanse me now from sin,
>     Fulfill Thy promise: make me pure within;
> Fill me with fire where once I burned with shame,
>     Grant my desire to magnify Thy name.
>
> Lord, take my life and make it all Thine own,
>     I want to spend it serving Thee alone;
> Take all my will, my passion, self and pride,
>     I now surrender, Lord, in me abide.
>
> O Holy Ghost, revival comes from Thee!
>     Send a revival, start the work in me!
> Thy Word declares Thou wilt supply our need,
>     For blessing now, O Lord, I humbly plead.

# Chapter 12

## THREEFOLD COMMITMENT

Dr. Harry Ironside, for whom I preached in 1935 in the Moody Church in Chicago, told the story of a Hopi Indian, giving testimony before a crowd of braves and squaws. The big man told his audience that before he was converted, he used to go to town on Saturday night and get drunk, and then his big black dog bit everybody. When Jesus Christ came into his life He gave him a big white dog which liked to help everybody. "But now," he said, "I have two dogs, and they often fight." A chief, sitting on the front seat, asked the important question: "Which dog winning?" Said the brave, after careful reflection: "Whichever dog that I say 'sic him' to."

There are some Christians who say that they can shoot that old black dog dead, but they agree that they can raise another black pup. There are some who say that the old black dog will live with them until the day they die. There are some who strive to starve the old black dog to death, or to chain him up. Whatever the views, the problem is: what can be done with the old black dog? What can be done about the carnal nature that still afflicts the Christian?

What to do about occasional lapses into acts of sin in the life of the believer has already been considered. If one confesses losing temper, he enjoys forgiveness, without a doubt. But what about persistent evil temper? Christians show concern much more about persistent sins, about recurring evil habits, and about temptations never overcome. Is there a remedy for this, or must one strive in vain as long as life shall last?

Salvation is threefold in its effects: first, the effect of justification is to deliver the believer from the guilt of sin; the effect of sanctification is to deliver the believer from the power of sin; whereas the effect of glorification is to deliver the believer from the very presence of sin.

When one by simple faith receives the Lord as Saviour, he is delivered from the guilt of sin; and when he meets Him face to face in death or rapture, he is delivered from the presence of sin; but between these two events he lives his life on earth in which the indwelling Holy Spirit seeks to deliver him from the power of sin. It is with such actual deliverance our thoughts are now concerned.

So much controversy has arisen about sanctification that the average Christian tends to leave the subject unresolved, or lives in total ignorance of its significance. And those who seem familiar with the doctrine expend their energies debating it from biased points of view instead of trying to relate it to the other aspects of salvation. "Hagios" in Greek is simply rendered "holy," or in its Latin form, "sanctified." And "to sanctify" is "to set apart," "to dedicate," "to consecrate," in the sacred sense of the service of God. About this definition, there is no controversy, but there is much debate about interpretations.

Years ago I addressed a class of theological students in Brisbane, capital of Queensland. I asked them: "What do we mean by sanctification?"

"Sanctification," a young lady answered, "is moment by moment, hour by hour, day by day, growth in grace."

A young man rose to offer an alternative: "Sanctification is the deeper blessing after conversion."

Another young man, a Scofield Bible under arm, declared: "Every believer is sanctified."

Within one minute or so, I had heard three apparently contradictory definitions of sanctification or holiness. And it seems that knowledgeable evangelical Christians are divided into three schools of thought, in reverse order: those who affirm that sanctification is the "position" of all believers; those who claim that sanctification is a "crisis" in the life of committed believers; and those who say that sanctification is a "process" - simply growth in grace in the life of normal believers. Positional sanctification is the view prevailing among followers of John Darby; critical sanctification is the general view found   among followers of John Wesley; progressive sanctification is the normal view of followers of John Calvin.

The school of thought which canonizes "saints" is not considered relevant. Not even Christ's apostles were ever designated "saints" by any sacred writer to distinguish them from ordinary believers, generally named "saints" regardless of their reputations. Many godly folk, in every generation or communion, brightly lighted up the Faith; but not a few thus canonized detracted from its glory.

Scripture warrants all three views of holiness, stated in positive terms, but any undue emphasis on any one of them without the balance of the other two results in harmful heresy. The doctrine must be taught with the same balance found in Scripture, which is its own best interpreter. Let us seek to illustrate the threefold application of the truth.

A friend of mine had lost a valued 16mm camera. Many months later he rediscovered it in a pawnshop window. On impulse, he quickly went into the shop, explaining to the pawnbroker that the camera in the window was his. Alas, he could not give proof of ownership, such as its serial number, and the pawnbroker was firm in his refusal to give it up unless the price was paid. So my friend declared he would go right home and get some money to redeem the camera. The pawnbroker said: "I'll set it apart for you."

When the amateur photographer returned home with the redeemed camera, he set time aside to dust it.

It worked unsatisfactorily, so he took the camera to pieces at a later date, and carefully cleaned and oiled the whole mechanism, polishing the metal and the leather parts until they looked like new. Even after that, he took the time to set aside the camera, keeping it in proper order, improving operation.

It should be obvious that in purchasing our redemption, the Lord set us apart, first of all. In that sense, therefore, we were sanctified even before we were redeemed. Once purchased, He cleansed us from the accumulated filth of sin. As time goes by, because our lives are not working very satisfactorily, He gives us an overhaul. Then, as He continues to use us, He keeps on cleansing us. Hence our sanctification is positional, critical, and progressive.

One realizes that handy illustrations sometimes blind the critical faculties of a Bible student. Too often a convenient illustration satisfies one's picture-sense and dulls one's analytical ability. Doctrines must not be grounded on easy illustrations. It is not enough to give an illustration unless it illustrates a Scriptural statement. The fact remains that usage of the Greek word "hagios" falls into three distinct, convenient categories in the New Testament: let us look for such statements in the Scriptures.

## Positional Sanctification

Is there Scripture for the claim that every true believer is sanctified from the moment of conversion? Yes, indeed! It is not hard to find.

Paul the Apostle wrote his first epistle to the church at Corinth, "sanctified in Christ Jesus, called to be saints." His strictures on them showed them to be far from saintly in the dedicated sense: they were so carnal that impurity, drunkenness, and fanaticism were tolerated in their midst. Yet he called them "saints," "sanctified in Christ Jesus," their bodies temples of the Holy Spirit.

A fisherman, washed overboard, left a young widow and a boy of eight in poverty. Their good pastor quietly opened a savings account in the name of the orphaned boy, adding to it occasionally as gifts were made. Ten years later, the boy won a scholarship in a university far to the south. The mother visited the pastor twice to see if funds for travel could be provided by the church, and was told twice to draw the boy's savings from the bank, a cruel joke, she thought. But before the deadline, she discovered the unknown credit, placed there by another hand. Had her boy earned the cash that he was now free to use? No, it was credited.

The first Corinthian letter places sanctification before justification, and sanctification before redemption (6:11 & 1:30). The Ephesian letter (4:24) refers to the new nature of believers, created in "true righteousness and holiness." The Apostle Peter's first letter (1:2) speaks of positional sanctification also, as does the Epistle of Jude.

Can this wonderful truth be twisted into heresy? This has happened too often by erroneous advocates who deny the need of holy living and ignore the other aspects of sanctification, critical or progressive, the practical holiness of condition rather than position.

A preacher in Los Angeles, of some renown, told me of an elder in his church, "a really good Bible teacher who taught a wonderful Bible class, rightly dividing the Word of Truth, able to smell a heresy a mile away." He had a fault; he had a weakness for women, misbehaving himself in the mountains every now and then. "He was certainly a real believer," the pastor said, "so we just had to admit that the old nature could not be defeated! So we put him back to teaching Bible class." I protested that such an elder would not have been allowed to teach in any congregation of mine unless he demonstrated true repentance.

## Critical Sanctification

Is there Scripture for the claim that a believer, after his conversion, may come to a place of complete commitment, a crisis of experience in living the Christian life?

The Apostle Paul, in his letter to the Romans

(12:1), appealed to them "by the mercies of God, to present your bodies as a living sacrifice, holy and acceptable to God, which is your spiritual worship." Someone may object that the verb "to present" could mean "bit by bit, moment by moment"; but this is not born out by the original Greek, which is in the aorist imperative tense, a Greek peculiarity signifying a point of action rather than continued action. In the C. B. Williams Translation, noted for its faithfulness in the shades of meaning in the Greek verbs, it is translated as "decisive dedication;" my own preference, "dedicated decisively," is supported by the veteran Greek grammarian Julius R. Mantey, of the Dana and Mantey Greek Grammar.

It seems to have been the experience of the most deeply spiritual Christians of my acquaintance to have made some definite spiritual progress immediately after conversion, in the glow of their first love, and then to have marked time or even gone down the grade until decline was recognized. Biographies of the world's most pious people reveal much the same graph of spiritual growth. New converts, enthused with new experiences, have not yet come to the conclusion of the Apostle Paul, "I do not understand my own actions. For I do not do what I want, but I do the very thing I hate." "Wretched man that I am! Who will deliver me from this body of death?"

The figure of speech, "this body of death," is believed to have been taken from a cruel Roman custom of chaining a murderer hand and foot to the corpse of his victim. And certainly the exclamation pictures for us the disgust that a Christian, possessing the new nature, finds in his spirit when he realizes that he is dragging around with him an odorous cadaver, the old nature which he detests.

The war between the old and new natures is real to every Christian just as soon as he starts to grow in grace. The Apostle Paul reminded the Corinthian church that they were not spiritual, but carnal Christians. The difference between them seemed to lie in whether they lived a life of victory or defeat, spirituality or carnality being clearly differentiated.

Biographies of departed saints and testimonies of living overcomers underline the fact that the unsatisfactory state of carnality generally provokes a crisis, whereby believers come to realize that God, who delivers from the guilt of sin through faith in Christ, is able to deliver from the very distressing power of sin as well.

At the historic Student Briefing Conference at Forest Home in the San Bernardino Mountains in 1949, I shared the platform with Billy Graham and Charles Templeton, both evangelists. Charles Templeton asked me whether or not I had experienced ups and downs in the Christian life before the crisis of commitment then described. I said yes. Then he asked me whether or not I still had ups and downs, and again the answer was yes. So he asked: "What difference does it make?" The question was sincere and friendly.

The difference, I explained, was that whereas the ups and downs of a carnal Christian are variations on a lowly level of living, the ups and downs of a committed Christian are variations of experience on a plateau of lofty consecration.

During World War II, my wife and I once rode by bus from San Antonio, Texas, south to Mexico City. Across the muddy Rio Grande we found the plains of northern Mexico dusty, dirty, hot, and mosquito-infested. Up and down we went, on dusty roads, through shabby towns, up and down but never out of the torrid heat of the "tierra caliente" of Mexico.

At long last, we reached the little town of Tamazunchale (nicknamed Thomas-and-Charlie by gringo tourists) where the road began to climb up through mountains to the high plateau of Mexico, the delightful "tierra temprada" where the air was clear, the nights cool, the mosquitoes few, the water pure, and the general conditions bracing. So we continued, up and down, but always higher than the plain, until we reached the capital in the "bowl of the gods."

At our lowest on the plateau, we were still two thousand meters higher than our highest on the plain.

The victorious life has its ups and downs, but at an elevation far removed from the depressing ups and downs of the carnal life. Yes, there is a plateau of Christian living, "heavens tableland."

Just as a Christian who stops at positional sanctification makes a heresy out of a blessed truth, so another one who stops at critical sanctification is guilty of a similar error. Some who rightly teach a crisis of commitment wrongly make it the achievement of a state of sinless perfection in which there is no further need of sanctifying grace.

I personally have never met a man who lived a sinless life. (I met a man who said that he had heard of one, his wife's first husband.) I have met saints who lived a life of victory over sin. I have met others who claimed to live a life entirely free from sin, but by sin they meant a breach of the Ten Commandments, not the New Testament definition of sin. The Scriptures teach that one who knows the right but fails to do it is guilty of sin; that whatsoever is not of faith is sin. Wesley called such omissions "involuntary transgressions" rather than "wilful sins." Be that as it may, the important question is: "Is it culpable?"

A speeding driver reached a traffic signal as the yellow caution light went on, but as he crossed the intersection line, the signal switched to red. Instead of braking, he coasted on, over the crossing. He informed the traffic cop that he had not driven on against the red; he had not driven, only coasted. He was guilty just the same.

## Progressive Sanctification

Just as positional sanctification is incomplete without a crisis of commitment, so the crisis is incomplete without a process following. Progressive sanctification is the hope of the believer once he has reached the higher plain.

It is not denied that recent converts grow in grace in their first love, and that ordinary Christians make headway in many areas of life. But if practical sanctification be regarded as deliverance from the power of known sin, it is apparent that only progressive sanctification can carry on.

As soon as Christians dedicate their lives completely to the Lord, the Spirit's search-light shows up another fault; when it is cleansed, some further light is given on another area. The moment a believer disobeys the leading of the Lord, he walks in darkness in that respect, not losing his commitment necessarily in other ways, although effects of disobedience tend to spread.

The weakness of the "growth in grace only" school is that it is assumed that growth is automatic, whereas it depends upon obedience. Obedience entails a series of crises, but there is always one in which the Christian first surrenders all of which he is aware. A boy of eight may dedicate his life completely; at the age of eighteen, his life involves dimensions hitherto unknown as sex begins to play its part; he must commit that problem to the Lord. At twenty-eight, he encounters problems making money in business, and must commit that also to the Lord. But whatever it may be, he cannot dedicate anything more than 100 percent, which is what he wished to do in first commitment.

The lives of saintly people seem to show that there was indeed a first time when they consciously yielded their all to God and that yieldedness was renewed from time to time. Obviously, they experienced both crisis and a process.

# Chapter 13

## FAITH IS THE VICTORY

The Epistle to the Romans, one of the greatest of all the tracts of Scripture, was written primarily to a company of believers of above-average spirituality, as the words following the salutation indicate: "I thank my God through Jesus Christ for all of you that your faith is spoken of throughout the whole world" (1:8).

### The Guilt of Sin

The first three chapters of the letter are devoted mainly to the doctrine of sin, summed up for the reader in the well-known text: "All have sinned and come short of the glory of God" (3:23).

This insistence upon the universality of sin may be put to a test anywhere, with the same result. I once talked with a Christian Scientist who declared that sin was no more than an illusion of the mortal mind, but he admitted that he suffered occasionally from that illusion. I once met an atheist who told me that sin was no more than falling short of one's own ideals, but he admitted that he fell short of his own ideals most of the time.

### Justification

Just as the first three chapters deal with sin, the next two discuss justification. Hence, the first verse of the fifth chapter states: "Therefore, since we are justified by faith, we have peace with God through our Lord Jesus Christ."

The average Christian thinks of justification as another term for forgiveness and so misses the meaning of this great word. Many years ago, I was driving with my friend Armin Gesswein through Pasadena, my mind more on the conversation than upon the traffic. I made what I thought was a full stop at a stop sign, and then pulled around into the boulevard crossing at right angles. A few seconds later, a traffic policeman overhauled me. He insisted that I had not stopped at the intersection, but admitted that I had very nearly come to a stop. As an act of grace, he said: "We'll forgive you this time," and allowed me to proceed. I had been forgiven, but I was not justified. How did I know? The traffic cop followed me; I was on probation.

Captain Alfred Dreyfus, an officer of the French Army, was falsely charged and wrongly imprisoned on Devil's Island. His friends secured a retrial in which the judge exonerated the prisoner and set him at liberty. Not at all satisfied, Dreyfus demanded and received from the French authorities all his back pay as well as the restoration of his rank as captain. He had been justified.

But someone may object: "Dreyfus was innocent, and was declared innocent. But I admit that I am guilty. How does God justify me?" In Romans 5:1 it is made clear that our justification is found in Christ: "Therefore, being justified by faith, we have peace with God through our Lord Jesus Christ." In the mystery of the atonement, God laid upon Him the iniquity of us all. Just as when a pastor, in sympathy with an erring youngster in his congregation, quietly takes up a collection and pays the fine, the boy going free, in the same way, we are not only forgiven, but we are justified, exonerated, treated as if we had not sinned at all. But it is important to notice in that key verse (5:1) that the transition from the low level of the guilt of sin to the high level of justification, being accounted blameless, is by faith and not by any effort on our part.

At the Jesuit University of Santa Clara, I was once asked: "Does your Bible teach that faith without works is dead?" I quickly agreed. "Then are we not saved by two things, by faith and by works?" "Not two things," I replied, "but by one, the faith that works. James, the brother of the Lord, asked rhetorically: 'If a man says he has faith, but has not works, can that kind of faith save him?' The answer is no!" My friends were still puzzled.

"Listen," I went on, "the friends next door to us are devout Irish Roman Catholics. They wanted to go to the wedding of relatives in Mexico but could not go because of the needs of a tiny infant. My wife volunteered: 'Leave the baby with us. Go and enjoy yourselves.' They demurred at first, but finally left the baby with us. That was good works, wasn't it? The reason Mrs. Orr did it was not because she thought that what Christ accomplished on the cross was only 90 percent effective, requiring 10 percent of good works to make the difference, but rather because she believed that what Christ accomplished on the cross was 100 percent effective and she was glad to do the good works just to thank Him."

So, the first five chapters of the Roman letter show that every last man born into this world faces the problem of the guilt of sin; and the answer to the problem surely is justification, which comes by faith, and works follow faith.

### Outline of the Epistle to the Romans

| Section | Subject | Key Verse | Pronoun |
|---|---|---|---|
| 1-3 | Guilt Of Sin | 3:23 | all |
| 4-5 | Justification | 5:1 | we |
| 6-7 | Power of Sin | 6:1 | we |
| 8-12 | Sanctification | 12:1 | you |

The first three chapters of the Epistle to the Romans show that everyone born into this world is a sinner; and chapters four and five show that some are justified by faith. The general conclusion is followed by a particular answer to the problem. But why did the Apostle Paul take the trouble to recapitulate these facts to a congregation whose faith was so well founded? A further problem?

## The Power of Sin

The subject of chapters six and seven is the problem of carnality in the life of the Christian, posed in the opening question of the sixth chapter: "What shall we say then? Are we to continue in sin that grace may abound? By no means!" In other words, because God has been so gracious as to forgive our sins and justify us freely, are we going to show our gratitude by imposing upon His grace? God forbid. That is antinomianism.

Gregory Rasputin taught a particularly obnoxious form of antinomianism. He proposed that as one who sins much must be forgiven much, the one who continues to sin with abandon enjoys more of God's forgiving grace than any ordinary sinner. There are many Christians who teach this in a milder way. I heard a Los Angeles pastor tell the Hollywood Christian Group that if any one of them awakened in Las Vegas with a woman not his wife and a flask of whiskey in the room, not to let it bother him. I advised the very opposite.

Suppose a great department store were to announce that it was prepared to forgive all outstanding debts at the start of the New Year. That might be good news for some widow whose husband had died and left her not enough money to pay her debts, but less honest folk would rush to order more on credit, in anticipation of running up an account to be automatically forgiven. Such license is both unreasonable and condemned.

So, the apostle asks, are we going to keep on sinning in order that we may enjoy more of God's forgiving grace? God forbid, yet it seems to be the experience of every Christian of my acquaintance that he continued occasionally to sin after his conversion to Christ.

Some teachers may relate Romans chapter seven to the unconverted. I once heard a radio preacher in Melbourne deliver an excellent evangelistic sermon using that chapter as his text. But let us put it to the test. In Romans 7:15, it is stated: "I do not understand my own actions, for I do not do what I want, but I do the very thing I hate." In 7:19, "I do not do the good I want, but the evil I do not want is what I do." In 7:22, "I delight in the law of God in my inmost self." And in 7:24, "Wretched man that I am! Who shall deliver me from this body of death?"

Either an unbeliever or a believer can say that sometimes he does not do the good that he wants to do, and sometimes does the very thing that he hates. But an unbeliever cannot say that he delights to do the will of God in his heart of hearts, nor can he declare that the struggle against such yielding to sin makes him wretched. Only the believer can say such a thing. Obviously, the believer was in the mind of the writer of the epistle.

How many believers can say that they do not do what they want, but that they often do the thing that they hate? I once asked a vast crowd of Indian church members whether they knew anyone who fulfilled these four points: one who knew what was right but did not always do it; one who knew what was wrong but sometimes did it; yet in his heart of hearts, he wished to please the Lord; and the struggle made him miserable. A little Indian woman jumped to her feet and declared: "My husband!"

Thus it is the carnal Christian who can say: "I do not understand my own actions, for I do not do what I want, but I do the very thing I hate." It is sin dwelling within the Christian which brings him to despair. But that does not mean that such a condition is inevitably permanent. Even in Romans chapter six, there is found both a promise and a method of dealing with the problem. The promise (6:14) tells us that sin will not hold dominion over us, for we are not under law but under grace. The method (6:11) tells us to reckon ourselves dead to sin and alive to God in

Christ.

## The Promise

It was Christ Himself who declared plainly that "whoever commits sin is the slave of sin," and so we talk of a man who is a slave to bad temper, a slave to strong drink, a slave to drugs, a slave to impurity. But the promise given in Romans assures us that no believer need any longer be a slave to sin. Why? Because he is not under law but under grace. Through grace, that sin need not hold dominion over him any more. He can break the power of sin in his life through the grace of Christ. As Charles Wesley said, "He breaks the power of cancelled sin and sets the prisoner free." This promise may become a reality.

The law does not help us to keep the law. I remember preaching in the great Moody Church in Chicago when three gangsters came in and stole the offering of those thousands of people. They were not apprehended, but had they been, one could not have imagined them telling the judge, "Your worship, honest, we did not know that we were breaking the law." Indeed they did, but the law does not help anyone to keep the law if he wishes otherwise. But believers are not under law but under grace, which means that they have now available to them all the unmerited help found in the Lord Jesus Christ.

A friend of mine, born in White Russia, emigrated in 1914 to the United States. His family being very poor, he was only given enough money for his railway fare to Liepaya in Latvia and his steamship fare across the Atlantic. His mother had provided him with a hamper full of cheese and bread sandwiches, in lieu of money for meals. By the time he reached Liepaya, he was very tired of cheese and bread.

On board ship, he heard the gong sound for meals, and saw the passengers troop below but he felt that the could not afford it, so he went up to the top deck to eat his bread and cheese in misery. Three days before the ship reached Halifax, he could bear it no more. He went to the cook and asked to be allowed to work in return for meals. The wily cook let him work for three days in return for the normal passenger fare. Only when he met his uncle in Chicago did he discover that his ticket included all the meals for which he had worked so hard.

The promise of Romans (6:14) assures believers that they need neither eat dry fare in disappointment nor work in perspiration in order to enjoy God's full provision. It is included in our salvation.

### The Method

The exhortation "Reckon yourselves dead to sin" may be interpreted in two different ways. The Calvinist may say: "God would not ask me to reckon myself dead if I were actually dead!" The Wesleyan may say: "God would not ask me to reckon myself dead if I were not actually dead." That seems to be a semantic problem.

On a Pacific island, I heard a couple of soldiers urge another to join them for a night of carousing. Busy writing home to his wife, he replied, "Count me out, fellows. I don't want to go!" and this was his way of reckoning himself dead.

A believer with a bad temper should remember that no one ever saw a corpse rise in a coffin to lose his temper. This reckoning of oneself dead to sin and alive to God is what Matthew Henry calls "mortification and vivification." One must be not only ready to act as dead to sin, but to act lively when an opportunity to serve God occurs.

"But," says the average Christian, "I have tried in vain to reckon myself dead to sin and alive to God. I am finding it difficult to live the Christian life."

It is not only difficult, it is actually impossible!

Why then does God expect us to live the Christian life? Because He has made provision. Just as a sinner cannot save himself, but may be saved nevertheless through the provision made in Christ, so the believer who cannot live the Christian life by himself may live victoriously through the provision God has made in the Spirit.

I have seen the Hindu pilgrims, on their way to a

"mela," lie on their bellies on the ground, make a mark with their fingernails, then stand up, step forward, put their toes where their fingers were, lie down, made another scratch, up-and-down, up-and-down, yard by yard, mile by mile, for a hundred miles. A pilgrim told me, "Sahib, I am trying to save my soul." When told that it is not only difficult to save one's own soul, but utterly impossible, the pilgrim asked: "Then why does God expect anyone to be saved?" The answer, of course, is that God has made provision for salvation, providing a Saviour; in fact, no one will be saved until he realizes that he cannot save himself.

In the same way, no believer can live the Christian life himself. Thomas a' Kempis wrote a Roman Catholic classic on "The Imitation of Christ," and Charles Sheldon published a Protestant classic about walking "In His Steps." There is, nevertheless, no Christian who can fully imitate Christ or walk in His steps. It is impossible. Why then does God expect anyone to live the Christian life? Because He has made provision, by providing the indwelling Holy Spirit.

### Sanctification

The eighth and twelfth chapters of Romans show that it is by the power of the Spirit that we may live a victorious life. At the moment of regeneration, we are "in Christ" at His high level; at the same moment, the indwelling Holy Spirit is in us at our low level of holiness which is the lot of a babe in Christ.

I heard the leader of a well-known Christian organization explain the privileges of the believer by taking his black leather-covered Testament, and using it as a symbol of the blackness of a sinners heart, and then completely covering it with his handkerchief, as Christ's righteousness.

The point was well-made. When I asked him whether or not anything happened to the blackness of a sinner's heart under the whiteness of the Saviour's grace, he hesitated and then said he had not thought that matter through. Such an important issue needs to be studied through and through.

I remember discussing with Dr. Henrietta Mears the problems of a friend who meant well, but was always giving way to his temptations. When rebuked, he protested: "You don't have the temptations that I have." "Poor fellow," said Miss Mears, "he sometimes says yes to temptation, and sometimes no, so he never knows what he is going to do. One who keeps on saying 'no' finds it less of a problem."

After unburdening his heart concerning the salvation of his own kinsmen, the Apostle Paul returns to the orderly course and, in the opening verses of the twelfth chapter, takes up again the main argument of his brief, coming to its climax. It is truly significant that the apostle uses the inclusive pronoun "all" in his first argument concerning universality of sin, the pronoun "we" in his second about justification and in his third about carnality, but switches to the pronouns "I" and "you" in his hearty exhortation: "I appeal to you therefore, brethren, by the mercies of God, to present your bodies as a living sacrifice, holy and acceptable to God, which is your spiritual worship." The only possible conclusion is that the apostle had already presented his whole personality to God, but the challenge implied that the Roman Christians had not so yielded.

It should be noted again that the common interpretation of Romans 12:1 seems to make of the infinitive "to present" a sort of daily dedication of one's life to God, whereas the Greek text makes it clear that the action is instantaneous. In other words, the verb "to present" in this case means to make a decisive dedication of the whole personality.

I remember, when participating in the meetings of an organization which encouraged its members world-wide to rededicate their lives in a monthly consecration service, standing to my feet to offer a vow of rededication. But nothing happened, for I was still holding onto my sins with one hand and trying to hold onto Christ with the other. The commitment of Christ is decisive; must not it be with me?

Imagine a seeking believer of the Keswick

Convention for the Deepening of the Spiritual Life, hearing the crowd sing: "I surrender all, all to Thee, my blessed Saviour, I surrender all." The believer knows that he has a bad temper a critical tongue, and a love of money; so he vows to God: "This year, I will surrender my bad temper, for it gets me into nothing but trouble. But I shall keep on criticizing unkindly until a year later, and then I'll quit. The year after that, I'll stop spending my money selfishly and begin to tithe in earnest." Would that be a decisive dedication, a complete commitment? No, it must be all at the moment of dedication, everything known.

The appeal, therefore, in the opening verse of Romans 12 is for decisive dedication, a yielding of the intellect, the will, and the emotions to God at a given moment rather than gradually, although the second verse urges the continual yielding of the personality day by day: "Be not conformed to this world, but rather be transformed by the renewing of your mind so that you may prove what is the will of God, what is good and acceptable and perfect."

The degree of yieldedness is governed by the degree of light, and the believer is expected to surrender his life to God only as he has light on the subject. Further light may mean further commitment, but a believer cannot dedicate more than his all at any given moment, therefore the first of all such commitments is unique, often renewed but never quite the same again.

It may be argued, against the crisis significance of the first verse of Romans 12, that the believer's life is full of crises. That is undeniable. But there must occur in the life of the believer a first time when, according to his light, he yields his life completely to God and finds himself proving what it is to know that "good and acceptable and perfect will of God" for himself, hitherto incompletely realized.

But the Christian must not stop at that point of dedication. Without a doubt, it is just as important to follow on in the life of total commitment as to make a decisive dedication. Yet far too many attempt to transform their lives by the renewing of their minds without first making a complete commitment to God.

Total commitment, decisive dedication, full surrender, the higher Christian experience, may be nullified by sin or disobedience. It is a crisis with a view to a process, and the moment the believer resists the work of the Spirit in raising him to still higher ground, he is in need of renewal of his commitment, whether it be intellectual, volitional, or emotional in nature. However, the appeal of Romans is for the initial yielding, then for continuance.

There is a truth hidden in the general outline of this epistle concerning the method to be implemented. Just as an unbeliever proceeds from the lower level of the guilt of sin to the higher level of justification by faith, which should be followed by works, so a believer proceeds from a lower level of the power of sin in his life to the higher level of complete commitment by faith, and works follow faith. Every blessing of the Christian life is by faith, by faith in the promises of God. Is it all unexpected that victorious Christian living should be also by faith? Surely faith is the victory that overcomes the world.

# Chapter 14

## THE HOLY SPIRIT

If the victorious life of the Christian depends upon the Holy Spirit, it is essential that the believer should learn something about the Holy Spirit, Who is (alas) almost unknown to many Christians.

I was lunching one day with a Presbyterian minister in the city of Belo Horizonte in Brazil. The door bell rang. It was a door-to-door fund raiser for a nearby parish church. He was collecting, he said, "por o Espirito Santo," for the Holy Spirit. To make conversation, my host inquired: "Who is the Holy Spirit, anyway?"

"Don't you know?" said the man. "The Holy Spirit is a bird, a pigeon. Some churches have it carved above the altar, but our padre noticed that we did not have the Holy Spirit in our church, so we are taking a collection during this Pentecost season to put the Holy Spirit in our church."

But that sort of ignorance prevails not only among the Latin American masses, but in surprising places in the United States and other English-speaking countries. In a Baptist church in Oregon, a lady asked me to explain the difference between the Holy Spirit and Santa Claus!

It is orthodox Christian doctrine that the Godhead truly subsists in three persons: the Father, the Son and the Holy Spirit. The doctrine of the trinity-in-unity is a mystery, that is, something beyond human explanation, yet capable of belief. It is first of all necessary to illustrate what is meant by a trinity-in-unity.

I once asked an audience for an apt illustration of this concept. A lady raised her hand, but her answer seemed so odd that I asked her to repeat it.

"An egg," she explained. "An egg has a shell, a white, and a yolk, three things yet one."

I demurred, telling her that the shell is made of calcium, the white of albumen, and the yolk of fat, three utterly different and unrelated things wrapped around each other, therefore impossible as an illustration of the triune God whose persons are identical in essence, in deity.

A pastor in Arizona suggested that the doctrine of the trinity could best be illustrated by the fact that he himself functioned as a father to his family, pastor to a congregation, and citizen of the state of Arizona. I demurred again, for his illustration was of a single person functioning in three ways at different times, hardly an illustration of the trinity.

Is there an apt illustration? I rather doubt it: the nearest illustration I can conjure up is that I know that I exist as a body, soul, and spirit; and yet I cannot say that either the body or soul or spirit is exclusively myself, for I am all three. I cannot explain this, but I believe it to be true.

In the same way, when we add up all that the Scriptures say about the Father, we find that He is the eternal Father; when we add up all that the Scriptures say about the Son, we find that He is the eternal Son; and when we add up all that the Scriptures say about the Spirit, we find that He is the eternal Spirit; and when we analyze all that the Scriptures say about God, we find that there is but one God.

The Scriptures attribute both deity and personality to the Father, Son, and the Holy Spirit, and the doctrine of the trinity-in-unity seems to be the only possible statement of the relationship of the persons in the Godhead, a doctrine which is beyond all human analogy.

## Personality

Christians are taught, therefore, that the Holy Spirit is a person, and yet one often hears presumably orthodox folk refer to the Spirit as "it" instead of "He." The only excuse for "it" lies in the fact that the Greek word for spirit is in neuter gender, an accident of language of the order of feminine gender in French for the moon. The Holy Spirit is someone more than mere influence emanating from God and yet that is what many Christians predicate in practice, if not in theory. What do we mean by personality? Obviously not a physical entity.

The average Christian is willing to assent to the doctrine of the personality of the Holy Spirit, but is seldom able to express what he means even by the word "person." Some say that the Holy Spirit is an individuality, therefore a person, forgetting that threes have individuality without personality.

By personality, we do not mean power. A motorist may drive up to a service station and request the attendant to fill up his tank with the spirit of petroleum, a dynamic power which has neither mind nor will nor emotion in the matter of the use of its power. The Holy Spirit is more than a spirit of power from God.

What are the marks of personality, distinguishing humans from things? The marks of personality are intellect, will, and emotion. A search of the Scriptures reveals that the Holy Spirit has intellect, will, and emotion, these attributes. For example, John 14:26: "He shall teach you all things," indicates that the Holy Spirit has intellect. Acts 16:6-7: "having been forbidden by the Holy Spirit" shows that the Holy Spirit has will. Ephesians 4:30: "Do not grieve the Holy Spirit of God," demonstrates that the Holy Spirit has emotion. These are the marks of personality; therefore the Holy Spirit is a person.

God created man in His own image, not a physical image but with intellect, will, and emotion. How do these in man compare with those in God? In man, these are limited; in God, they are infinite. The sum total of scripture verses suggest that the Holy Spirit is a self-conscious being, who possesses intellect, will, and emotion infinitely.

## Intellect

How does the intellect of the Holy Spirit compare with the intellect in man? Albert Einstein possessed an IQ of 209; What would be the comparable figure for the Holy Spirit? 1,000? 1,000,000? Is there a figure? Yes, indeed: infinity. If then the Holy Spirit, possessing all wisdom and all knowledge, never making a mistake, is Infinite Intellect, the sooner Christian folk learn to defer to His superiority the better, to subordinate their puny intellects to the mighty wisdom of the Spirit.

## Will

The same is true concerning will. One admires the will and purpose of a man who truly triumphs over adversity by sheerest effort of will. But the strongest will on earth is inferior to the will of the Holy Spirit, whose purposes are infinitely grander than all the purposes of mankind. The Holy Spirit has been placed in charge of the work of God on earth, and He knows what He is doing; His purposes are clear, and His plans will be fulfilled. He is Lord of the harvest, supreme in revival, evangelism, and missionary outreach. Without His consent, all other plans are bound to fail. It behooves us Christians to fit our tactical operations into the plan of His strategy, which is the reviving of the Church and awakening of the people, for the evangelization of the world and teaching of His people, that His Kingdom may come and His will be done on earth as it is in heaven.

## Emotion

Less appreciated in the thinking of the Christian is the infinite emotion of the Holy Spirit. Emotion is a powerful force in the lives of human beings, often surpassing both intellect and will. The attitude of a parent to his child is not based on calculating intellect or grim determination, but upon emotion of parental affection. It requires neither mental effort nor wilful purpose to love one's own offspring. The Holy Spirit loves the offspring of God, all the children of creation, but more so the children of God through faith in Christ. This love is a driving force to accomplish great good for us, all the days of our life and evermore.

At the same time, the Holy Spirit hates all sin and all disobedience, and is as ready to chasten us as a loving parent is to discipline his child. But the motion of the Holy Spirit is stronger than human emotion, and is not at all so fickle. It fortifies that of an ordinary Christian who, filled with the Spirit, finds himself capable of loving people for whom he had not a glimmer of love previously.

In concluding that the Holy Spirit is a person, of infinite intellect, will, and emotion, it is also wise to recognize that the same Scriptures which emphasize His personality are the source of all teaching concerning His deity.

## Deity

In what ways is God always distinct and different from all His creatures? God is eternal, but He gives to us eternal life; God is a spirit, but He made us living spirits also. In what ways is God always different?

It is conceivable that a superior being could exist with intellect, will and emotion greater than ours, yet be less than deity. How then do we know that the Holy Spirit is God. God is omnipotent, omniscient, and omnipresent. Angels are not all-powerful, all-knowing, and everywhere-present. Men are not omnipotent, omniscient, and omnipresent. Nor are the beasts of the field or the trees of the forest. Is there Scripture to suggest that the Holy Spirit in Himself possesses omnipotence, omniscience, and omnipresence?

There are references in Scripture to the Holy Spirit's creative power: "The Spirit of God was moving over the face of the waters" (Genesis 1:2) as He participated in creation. Human beings can make things, but cannot create anything. That work of God is attributed to the Spirit.

"What person knows a mans thoughts except the spirit of the man which is in him? So also no one comprehends the thoughts of God except the Spirit of God," (1 Corinthians 2:11). Only God can comprehend the thoughts of God, and this comprehension is attributed to the Holy Spirit.

There are references in Scripture to His omnipresence: "Whither shall I flee from thy Spirit?" (Psalm 139:7). Only God is omnipresent, therefore this further evidence of deity is added to the attributes of the Holy Spirit.

There is equal rank given the Holy Spirit, with the eternal Father and the eternal Son (2 Corinthians 13:14), and the Scripture also equates identity of the Holy Spirit and God (Acts 5:3-4). There are other arguments.

Thus we have two important conclusions to reconcile: the Holy Spirit is a distinct personality, and He is deity. The doctrine of the trinity-in-unity is the only possible solution of the problem, a doctrine capable of statement and belief, but beyond human explanation.

### Ministry

The Lord Jesus told His disciples (John 16:7-14) "It is to your advantage that I go away, for if I do not go away, the Counsellor will not come to you; but if I go, I will send Him to you. And when He comes, He will convict the world of sin and of righteousness and of judgment: of sin, because they do not believe in Me; of righteousness, because I go to the Father, and you will see me no more; of judgment, because the ruler of this world is judged. I have yet many things to say to you, but you cannot hear them now. When the Spirit of truth comes, he will guide you into all truth; for he will not speak on his own authority, but whatever he hears he will speak, and he will declare to you the things that are to come. He will glorify me, for he will take what is mine and declare it to you."

Thus is announced the ministry of the Holy Spirit, toward the world, toward believers, and toward the Christ.

It is significant to note His ministry toward the world, first convicting them of sin. Many people seem to think that this is the work of the conscience. But conscience is not absolute. It does not tell a man what is right and what is wrong, but rather reminds him what he believes to be right and what he believes to be wrong at a given time.

The Holy Spirit has absolute standards. He convicts folk of sin, using the Word of Scripture to do so, or awakening the conscience directly. He shows the sinner the sinfulness of sin. He exposes the final sin of unbelief.

The Holy Spirit also convicts of righteousness. I heard Dr. Henrietta Mears illustrate this point to a group of young ladies. A housewife decided to spend the morning cleaning up, soon becoming untidy herself. The front doorbell rang, much to her dismay, for there was a friend dressed in her best clothes. It was not necessary for the visitor to point out how untidy the housewife looked; the immaculate clothes of her visitor made her realize her own untidiness. So also the Holy Spirit presents the righteousness of Christ which, in the days of His earthly ministry, never failed to convict men of their shortcomings.

The Holy Spirit also convicts men of judgment. Men who have no fear of anything else may tremble when the Spirit of God warns them of their fate, to share the eternal doom of perdition, the eternal damnation of the devil and his host.

The Holy Spirit likewise convicts believers of carnality, of sanctification, and of the judgment seat of Christ. All obedient Christians are guided by Him into the truth.

Someone says: "Is not the Scripture the all-sufficient guide?" A short conversation with a heretical cultist will dispose of that fallacy. Scripture may be twisted, as the apostle once declared. I walked along the corridor of the Seattle Pacific College dormitories and heard a group of younger men discuss a chapter which I had written. One of them gave it a Calvinistic interpretation; another gave it a Wesleyan interpretation; but the third interpreted it quite extraordinarily. I was asked to explain, which I did to the satisfaction of the Presbyterian and the Methodist, but not the satisfaction of the sophomore, who asked: "Dr. Orr, are you sure that you meant it that way?" I assured him that I was sure that I was sure.

"Jim," he said to the Presbyterian, "you have had your say, and Joe," he said to the Methodist, "you have had yours. So let me have my say. Let me tell you what I feel Dr. Orr must have meant when he wrote his book."

But the author ought to know better what he meant when he wrote his book, allowing for any ambiguity; and the Holy Spirit alone can best interpret the sacred Word, which He inspired the writers to formulate. The Holy Spirit makes the Scripture come alive to committed readers.

It is the grandest work of the Holy Spirit to make Christ real to us, One whom we have never seen, and to glorify Him in a thousand ways. Frail mortals tend to glorify their own accomplishments, but the Spirit of God directs the glory to its rightful end, so that all may sing: "Worthy art Thou, our Lord and God, to receive glory and honor and power, for Thou didst create all things, and by Thy will they existed and were created," (Revelation 4:11).

Throughout the prophetic writings of the Old Testament runs the promise of the Messiah, God's anointed. Another promise parallels that theme, for, when the Apostle Peter at Pentecost told the multitude that "the promise is to you, and to your children, and to those who are afar off, and to as many as the Lord our God shall call," he was referring to the promise of the Holy Spirit given in the Old Testament and there fulfilled.

The promise of the Spirit was generally given in figures of speech: "I will pour waters on him that is thirsty, and floods on the dry ground" (Isaiah 44:3);

"Come from the four winds, O breath, and breathe upon these slain that they may live" (Ezekiel 37:9); and "I will pour out my Spirit upon all flesh, and your sons and your daughters shall prophesy, your old men dream dreams, and your young men shall see visions" (Joel 2:28).

This mighty vitalizing Spirit of God has been promised to the believer, as in the words of the Lord Jesus Himself: "He who believes in Me, as the Scripture has said, Out of his vitals shall flow rivers of living water" (John 7:38).

# Chapter 15

## THE SPIRIT AND THE BELIEVER

In His conversation with Nicodemus, the Lord Jesus no less than three times referred to being born of the Spirit (John 3), identifying this regeneration by the Spirit with being born again. It seems clear that every true Christian is regenerated by the Holy Spirit.

Because some professed Christians regard involuntary baptism as regeneration, while others use the term for the feeblest resolve to turn over a new leaf, it should be stated that the only evidence of the new birth is the new life.

In his first letter to the Corinthians, the Apostle Paul stated clearly that every true Christian is indwelt by the Holy Spirit. The Christians to whom he wrote were far from perfect, yet the apostle told them that their bodies were temples of the Holy Spirit (1 Corinthians 3:16).

Indwelling must not be confused with full possession. The Spirit of God acts as an ambassador of Christ in the life of a carnal Christian, but as viceroy in the life of a spiritual believer. The indwelling Spirit has His place in the home of the Christian soul, but every room in the house is available to Him in the home of a Spirit-filled believer.

The teaching of the Letter to the Romans makes it clear that every true Christian is assured by the Holy Spirit. The Spirit Himself bears witness with our spirit that we are the children of God (Romans 8:16). This is the doctrine of the assurance of salvation, believed ardently by Lutheran, Anglican, Calvinist, Wesleyan, and every evangelical, and by some of evangelical persuasion in unreformed circles. It is true that sometimes nominal members of professedly evangelical denominations admit a lack of assurance, but this is due to unfamiliarity with the doctrines of their faith.

Again, the Spirit is the witness, because the Spirit is the truth. I remember a child running home to mother, saying that some mischief-makers had said that he was not her little boy. "Of course you are," said the mother.

"How do you know, mamma?" he asked.

"I was there when you were born," she assured him.

"He who believes in the Son of God has the testimony in himself" (First John 5:7,10). The assurance is subjective, but it is always based upon an assurance of the Holy Scripture. An old Scottish lady was asked how she knew she was truly born again, and she replied: "It is better felt than telt!" It certainly is better felt than explained. No one can tell a young man in love whether or not his love is the real thing, for only he can tell in his own soul. The assurance of salvation is a conviction wrought in the human spirit by the Spirit of God. It may be possible for a man to become a believer in Christ and suffer from a time lag in receiving the assurance of salvation, as in the case of John Wesley; but conversely it is hazardous for anyone without spiritual assurance to claim to be a Christian.

Every true Christian is sealed by the Holy Spirit. The Ephesian Christians were warned not to grieve the Holy Spirit of God, in whom they were sealed for the day of their redemption (Ephesians 4:30). And who were sealed? Those who had heard the Word of truth, the good news of their salvation, and had believed in Christ (1:13). The Corinthian Christians were told much the same thing (2 Corinthians 1:22) about the seal of the Spirit. The Greek word for seal, common in the Septuagint and contemporary documents, is used for a legal mark of ownership or a closure of sale.

Every true Christian is guaranteed by the Holy Spirit, a truth taught in the same two letters (2 Corinthians 1:22 and 5:5 and Ephesians 1:14). The Greek word for guarantee or earnest is a Phoenician business term with the same significance as the modern term "down-payment." The reference in Ephesians is illuminating, for it states that the promised Holy Spirit is the guarantee of our inheritance until we acquire possession of it. A further illustration of a nonbusiness nature is the engagement ring, which is the token of a promised marriage until the union is complete. So the Holy Spirit in our hearts is the heavenly engagement ring, or the down-payment on the eternal inheritance.

Every true Christian has been baptized by the Holy Spirit into the body of Christ. The Apostle Paul makes this great doctrine clear in the first letter to the Corinthians (12:13) and includes everyone in Christ. Baptism in water is but a symbol of the baptism by the Spirit into the body of Christ, made possible by His own baptism of suffering on Calvary.

But there has been great confusion in the minds of many Christians regarding this baptism by the Holy Spirit into the body of Christ and the enduement of power or filling of the Holy Spirit, which certain Christians, with some Scripture references to quote, call the "baptism with the Spirit," a term used by Finney, Moody, Booth, Murray, Torrey, and a majority of nineteenth century evangelical leaders till reaction against emerging Pentecostalism made the term a matter of debate, until this day.

It is clear that the reference in the first letter to the Corinthians deals with the experience of the believer at his regeneration, when by faith in Christ he receives the Holy Spirit who baptizes him into the body of Christ. Let us call that experience the baptism of incorporation by the Spirit. The prediction of John the Baptist, reported by Matthew (3:11), Mark (1:8), Luke (3:16), John (1:33), that one who was coming after him would baptize believers in the Spirit (the Greek preposition is "en" just as in 1 Corinthians

12:13) was fixed and dated by the ascended Christ (Acts 1:5) and was referred to retrospectively by Peter (Acts 11:16); and in the latter two instances a relation to the enduement of power is made, the option of believers so incorporated.

Nowhere in the Acts or Epistles, written after Pentecost, is the term "baptized with the Spirit" used to describe the experience of any individual Christian, or to urge such an individual Christian to seek an enduement of power from on high. The word used in all post-Pentecostal cases about an individual is the word "filled" or "full." At Pentecost, it is true, one might say that all the disciples were baptized by the Spirit in a fulfillment of John's prediction, but the word used is "filled." Likewise, at Caesarea, also by inference, it might be said the whole company of Gentile believers was baptized with the Spirit, but the narrative does not say so directly.

These observations lead one to conclude that the better term to use to describe the enduement of power is the term "filling" rather than "baptism." Nevertheless, there may be a connection between the two terms when used for a reference to the enduement of power of the Spirit. A glass set in a sink may be quarter-filled with water, but it is not immersed. Neither can it be described as immersed when it is half-full, or three-quarters full, or full to the brim. And only when the vessel is filled to overflowing is there, in the real sense of the word, an immersion or a baptism. I take it that when individual Christians are filled to overflowing with the Spirit, there could be a baptism of the whole company with the Spirit.

Some good people, in their eagerness to help others into a place of power, ask the question: "Have you had your baptism?" by which they mean the enduement of power and not the baptism by the Spirit into the body of Christ. This is non-scriptural phraseology and misses a more germane question. In the military forces, to decide soldier's status, we asked men not "Have you had your honeymoon?" but "Are you married?" It is much better to ask a believer, "Are you totally committed to God?" remembering that no one in the New Testament testified: "I am filled with the Spirit," but that this was said by other observers of him.

To summarize these conclusions on a difficult subject, one may say that every true Christian is regenerated and indwelt, assured, sealed and guaranteed, and baptized by the Spirit, but he may or may not be filled with the Spirit.

# Chapter 16

## "BE FILLED WITH THE SPIRIT"

Into the heart of each obedient Christian there comes an intense yearning not only for victory over sin, but for power for service; and Christians in every generation, in every country, and in every denomination, have been aware of this desire.

The Lord Jesus said: "Blessed are those who hunger and thirst for righteousness, for they shall be satisfied." It seems inconceivable that the Lord of a perfect salvation would not make provision for every need of His children. There must be a way to purity and power.

On the last day of the feast, the Lord Jesus told the multitudes: "He who believes in Me, as the Scripture has said, Out of his heart shall flow rivers of living waters." The Greek word translated "heart" is a collective singular noun which encompasses all the vital organs of the body, hence "heart," "inmost being," "vitals," or "vitality." Therefore, it is appropriate to render the promise, "He who believes in Me, as the Scripture has said, Out of his vitality shall flow rivers of living water." The promise repeats the Old Testament prediction of living water.

Does this mean that every believer sends forth rivers of living water flowing from his vitality? Hardly. This is the option of every Christian, but alas how very few avail themselves of this promise. Christians from whose inmost being there flows a river of blessing are but few and far between, yet there are enough of them to be witnesses to the reality of the enduement with power from on high.

Elizabeth and Zechariah, parents of John the Baptist, were filled with the Spirit, and their offspring was filled with the Spirit from his mother's womb. His ministry is understandable only in the light of the filling of the Spirit.

The Lord Jesus Himself, being full of the Holy Spirit, was led into the desert to face the attack of Satan at the outset of His ministry; but He returned in the power of the Spirit. These facts are recorded for us by the physician Luke, who seemed to delight to record all such infillings of the Spirit, both in his first treatise and in his second, which ought to be designated "The Acts of the Spirit."

Before His ascension, the Lord Jesus announced the soon to be realized baptism of the Spirit, the beginning of the fulfillment of all the promises of the new dispensation of the Spirit given in the Old Testament.

In the Acts of the Apostles, the first outpouring of the Holy Spirit occurred in the upper room at Pentecost, when Peter and the other ten, together with Matthias and Joseph, and Mary the mother of Jesus, and the women who were following the Lord, and a large company of His disciples, about one hundred and twenty in all, were all filled with the Holy Spirit, and witnessed dynamically.

The effect upon Peter was startling. This disciple, who had denied his Lord with oaths and curses, stood up with the eleven and preached the first great evangelistic sermon of the Christian faith. As a result of this and the others' witness, about three thousand of the inquirers were added to the church that day. The only explanation was that the remarkable Person, the Holy Spirit of unlimited intellect, will, and emotion had taken possession of the intellect and will and emotion of Peter and his colleagues, using their whole personalities to reach the multitudes with such convicting power that they were cut to the heart.

This incident, and indeed every other one that is recorded, emphasizes that the filling of the Holy Spirit is for service. In each instance, the infilling was followed by some strong action. This was indeed the fulfillment of the promise of the risen Christ: "You shall receive power when the Holy Spirit has come upon you." Power for what? "You shall be my witnesses." The filling of the Holy Spirit was not, is not, and will not be given merely for spiritual ecstasy, but always for service.

But not only was the Apostle Peter filled on that glorious day of Pentecost: they were all filled, John and James and Andrew and Philip and Thomas and Bartholomew and Matthew and James and Simon and Judas and Matthias, all apostles; as well as James, Joses, Judas and Simon, the brothers of Jesus; and Mary the mother of Jesus, Mary of Magdala, Mary of Bethany, Martha, Joanna, Susanna, Salome, and other women who had been with the Lord in His ministry; a score of these who were filled are named for us, but a hundred others remain unnamed. The empowering of the unnamed disciples is an encouragement indeed to every humble Christian who might be tempted to think that the power from on high is meant only for those whom God intends to exalt to leadership, for when Peter declared that "This is what was predicted by the Prophet Joel," he revealed that "sons and daughters" were prophesying aplenty at Pentecost, not himself only.

Luke as historian revealed that the Apostle Peter was filled again with the Holy Spirit, some days later. From a reading of the narrative it is unwarranted to suggest that the Apostle had backslidden in the meantime. From this fact it can be seen that the filling of the Holy Spirit is not given as a restorative from backsliding but that it has a direct bearing upon immediate service. One might add, from observation of modern saints, that there appear to be times of relaxation and rest in between times of enduement with power, relaxation without any grieving of the Spirit.

The fullness of the Holy Spirit is under the sovereignty of the Spirit rather than that of the recipient. And the normal characteristics of the recipient are not superseded, as is the case in demon possession when derangement occurs.

Another large company of Christians was filled with the Holy Spirit (Acts 4:31) and spoke the Word of God with boldness. As the numbers of the believers had exceeded ten thousand, it became necessary to choose seven deacons to help the apostles in their administrations. All seven, Stephen and Philip, Prochorus and Nicanor, Timon and Parmenas and Nicolaus, were chosen as men "full of the Holy Spirit," their initial filling a matter of conjecture.

The martyr Stephen, to whom the evangelist Luke refers so many times as full of faith, full of grace, full of power, full of wisdom, full of the Holy Spirit, filled with the Holy Spirit, delivered an unexcelled message of power to a hostile mob who finally stoned him to death, death overtaking him while he was yet filled with the Spirit (Acts 6:3,5,8,10; 7:55).

The glorious deaths of the martyrs are inexplicable apart from the filling of the Holy Spirit. At the beginning of the 1939-1945 World War, a Korean Presbyterian pastor was seized by the Kempetai, the Japanese security police. The chief inquisitor asked him, to his surprise, if he believed in the second coming of Jesus Christ. He said that he did. Why, he was asked, would Christ return? He explained that Christ would come to judge all men. Why? Because all men are sinners. Would Christ judge His Imperial Majesty the Emperor? Carefully paying respect to the Emperor, he affirmed that the Emperor too would be included among the sinners unless he became a Christian. For this boldness, he was beaten up. The police chief asked him if he knew how Christ had died. He was crucified, said the pastor. Then, said the tormentor, that would be how the stubborn pastor would die. The Korean knew that the secret police were capable of carrying out their threats, but instead of feeling deadly fear he was possessed of a sudden and overwhelming sense of joy that he was accounted worthy to suffer as the Saviour had suffered. Instead of crucifying him, they suspended him by the thumbs roped to a hook in the ceiling, with his arms behind his back and his toes barely grazing the ground. He was in physical agony, but his heart was filled with joy, and he was so filled with the Spirit that he testified ardently to the guards. He was cut down, thrown out, and nursed back to health by his flock.

The evangelist Philip, full of the Holy Spirit, went down to the city of Samaria, where multitudes received Christ. The same empowering Spirit took Philip away from the scene of his successes, down to a dirt road in the desert where he won a wayfaring Ethiopian official to Christ and baptized him in a pool there.

There are those who consider evangelists charlatans, and some (sad to say) are false, but objective Christians studying the records are compelled to agree that there are evangelists who seem to possess a power of persuasion beyond explanation. Such soul-winning is a gift of God (Ephesians 4:11), empowered by the recurring filling of the Holy Spirit. They are filled for this service.

The Apostle Paul, converted as Saul of Tarsus on the road to Damascus, was visited by Ananias of Damascus that he might be "filled with the Spirit." The greatest ministry of all the apostolate followed, expressed in the greatest missionary enterprise of all time.

As one who has visited almost all the mission fields, and one who has directed the researches of missionaries in mid-career, it is easy to express the opinion that those who give up home and friends and fortune to plant the faith among people of alien tongue and culture are the front-line heroes of the greatest calling on earth. There are some who have failed to persevere, but the greatest are those who went out in the power of the Spirit. And greatest of all are those who sought that power for their impossible tasks.

It is clear from Scriptural records and historical

details that the filling of the Holy Spirit was given for preaching, for witnessing, for evangelism, for personal work, for missionary enterprise, for discernment, for martyrdom.

There are some who have said that the filling of the Holy Spirit was only for early apostolic days, a notion without either Scriptural or historical support. In the nineteenth century, Charles G. Finney, Dwight L. Moody, William Booth, Hudson Taylor, and a host of other great leaders testified of the filling of the Holy Spirit. In the twentieth century, there have been Evan Roberts, Reuben Torrey, Wilbur Chapman, A.B. Simpson, Lionel Fletcher and so many others whose work has been happily endorsed.

On the mission fields, wherever there has been spiritual revival and great awakening, there have been outstanding examples of the filling of the Holy Spirit. The best and the most-used Christians known to me at home or abroad have been men who have testified to a deeper experience of the filling of the Holy Spirit. The choicest women serving God have given the same testimony to me, whether the daughter of General Booth best known as La Marechale, or Henrietta Mears, or Corrie ten Boom, or Marta Carlson.

It is a remarkable fact that the end of the nineteenth and the beginning of the twentieth century were marked by a worldwide movement of prayer in all denominations which stressed the work of the Holy Spirit. It was followed by a worldwide revival/awakening in every country where there was an evangelical witness. The general movement was charismatic in the general sense of the gifts, but not in the particular sense of glossolalia.

Out of the widespread movement came a minority seeking a renewal of the apostolic gifts, with greater emphasis on healing and on tongues-speaking. This was the Pentecostal aftermath of the early 1900's Awakening. The churches in general rejected the Pentecostal emphasis, driving out and persecuting its advocates. Rejected by the churches, many Pentecostals were driven in upon themselves, and an extreme fanaticism developed among some who brought discredit upon the others. Pentecostalism thrived among less-educated classes, as happened a century earlier in Methodism; but while many choice men of God identified themselves with the movement, there was no great scholar such as John Wesley to conserve the fruits by insight and education.

Alas, in forty years of decline, the doctrine of the filling of the Holy Spirit suffered not only from neglect and from contradiction, but from fanatical teaching and practice that scared away many sincere seekers.

Two generations after the rise of the movement, not only had the Pentecostal denominations settled down and gained maturity, but another charismatic movement began to affect the historic churches, again with some fanaticism but with much more acceptance; and the filling of the Spirit became a live concern to increasing numbers once more.

# Chapter 17

## THE POWER AND THE GIFTS

With every personality throughout the world distinct, and every last conversion being very different, it is surprising that the question should occur so frequently: "What is the filling of the Spirit like?" as if it could be stereotyped.

The Holy Spirit has been represented as fire and wind and water, all elements of nature, so it is appropriate to speak of spiritual experience with God as burning as a fire, as bending as a hurricane, as gentle as a well of water, bubbling up from deepest depths, becoming "like a river glorious in its perfect peace."

The stated purpose for the filling of the Holy Spirit is one of power for service, hence the conclusive evidence of the filling of the Spirit is power in service, power unmistakably of God and not purely physical or psychic power. So, when a believer, known to have been seeking for a filling of the Spirit, is observed to have developed greater power in turning sinners from their sin to righteousness, or leading other saints into profounder truths, or simply glorifying Christ by prayer or praise, it should be conceded that such power presents a proof of infilling by the Spirit.

While it may be said that power is unspecific in some instances, the power is generally given in some specific gift. In the Ephesian letter (4:11), four gifts are listed: apostle, prophet (said to be defunct), evangelist, and pastor teacher, the latter two combined though each can be found active separately, "for the equipment of the saints, for the work of the ministry, for building up the body of Christ."

The office of apostle in its strictest sense had died away when those who witnessed the life and death and resurrection of their Lord had left this scene; it continues only in the sense of the missionary church-planter, Hudson Taylor being an outstanding illustration.

Completion of the canon of New Testamental writings minimized a need for prophets in the church, the gift itself continuing as simple exhortation, or more dramatically in one delivering a message to the body of believers, as did Evan Roberts in the Welsh Revival.

Some serous expositors maintain, incredibly it seems, that the gift of an evangelist has likewise ceased to be. The work of the evangelists, Wesley, Moody, Graham, to name a few, should contradict the notion out of hand. In one sense, believers all should be evangelists or witnesses, but God has given great persuasive powers to chosen men.

More and more today, the pastors of many congregations are led to reassess their call and gift, not as the single voice of proclamation in the church but to equip the saints themselves for works of ministry in building up the church. Two great pastors of today, Halverson in Washington and Smith in Costa Mesa, have found their call in putting folk to work in their own vineyard. And although some pastors have a teaching gift, it seems to magnify in others to the point of genius; that was Henrietta Mears' gift in Sunday School, and many a professor's in his graduate class.

The greatest planters, prophets or evangelists, pastors, and teachers of the Word, have been believers who in full commitment sought the filling of the Spirit. I could give a lengthy list of names. I also know of ones who showed their gift as helper or administrator, as listed in Paul's first epistle to Corinthians, some too shy to speak but not too shy to work, and others with a touch for management, a blessing in the church or missionary society.

In his first epistle to Corinthians (12:4-11), the Apostle Paul records nine gifts of God, imparted by the Spirit as He wills. Unlike the fruit produced by an infilling, the gifts are not presented as collective singular, and no believer is able to assert that if he has one, he has all. In fact, the Holy Spirit allocates these gifts "to each one individually;" and, in elucidating their relationship, comparison is made with members of the human body, related and dependent one upon the other, so that the foot is indispensable to eyes and hands. So, in Christs body, gifts are given, making members each depend the one upon the other.

These nine gifts are wisdom, knowledge, faith, healing, power, prophesy, discernment, tongues, and interpretation. The Spirit's gifts are supernatural endowments, not to be at all confused with ordinary talents. A Christian worker may be talented in singing, but no doubt his voice had been as much esteemed in unconverted days in worldly entertainment, or could be so today. Another worker's gift may lie in public speaking, but his talent could be used as readily in party politics. The Spirit's gifts are supernatural.

The gift of wisdom is expressed in trenchant insights given by the Spirit to believers. It is wisdom far beyond or different from all human wisdom. Of all the men I met, I most esteemed the gift of C.S. Lewis, Oxford don, whose insight into truth his hearers thought uncanny.

The gift of knowledge has been recognized by experts such as Donald Gee, as accumulated knowledge of the ways of God, disclosed within His Word or in His leadings. G. Campbell Morgan most impressed me with his knowledge of the Holy Scriptures just as Julius Mantey showed his gift in handling them in Koine Greek: a gift exercised with diligence.

Some charismatic leaders now define this gift as

some uncanny knowledge of conditions or events beyond their own experience, such as awareness of diseases that afflict mankind. I know of instances supporting such interpretation, and I also know of humbugs who inform two thousand people that among them is a victim of migraine headaches, a guess that anyone could make. The test of such predictions surely is the question whether such selected individuals afterwards attest their healing.

The gift of faith is not enlargement merely of the faith possessed by every Christian, but it is special gift for special tasks, such as the faith of Hudson Taylor to reach out to all of China with the Gospel, or George Muller's faith in caring for his orphans, and the like. Every Christian has some faith, but the gift of faith is meant to benefit the church at large and bring great glory to the name of Christ.

The gift of healing is a gift enabling its recipient to help to health and wholeness those who suffer in the body or the mind. In my opinion, healing is available to Christians in at least four ways. First, God seems to bless the use of means, for in earth are minerals and herbs upon the field, with healing powers; yet some are so fanatical that they will not even use a medical prescription. Secondly, God seems to bless the ministry of Christian nurses and physicians, giving opportunities exceeding those of pastors on occasion; yet some are so fanatical that they will not call a doctor. (Luke the physician did not cease to practice his profession.) Third, God seems to trust with special powers the elders of the church to pray for sick believers; yet in most denominations, prayers for the sick are often utterly neglected. And fourth, God seems to grant unusual gifts of healing to anointed individuals for public ministry. In this category, there have been too many scandals on account of exploitation, overstated claims and such like. Temptations must be great among these gifted few.

Once I debated an outstanding atheist who was a professor of the philosophy of science. He stated that it was not unusual that a great religious leader such as

Jesus Christ should have been credited with several psychosomatic healings. He obviously was not as qualified in history as in the fields of science and philosophy to voice such silly observations. Yet so many uninformed observers seem to think that only illness due to sick imagination (real to those who suffer) have been cured by the power of prayer. This is far from being the case.

When visiting South Africa, I often stay with a valued friend, a noted obstetrician in Pretoria. Paul Bremer told me once that Mrs. Elsie Salmon, gifted wife of a Methodist minister, visited wards of the Pretoria General Hospital to pray for the sick. Among them was a patient of his in terminal cancer. After prayer, the woman claimed that she was healed, and wanted to return to home and family on an eastern Transvaal farm. The doctors were upset, thinking she needed morphine to face her days of dying rather than false hope stirred up by some misguided amateur. Although he had a skilled pathologist's report on file, my doctor friend insisted on reexamining the woman, and simply could not find a trace of cancerous growth. The woman went back to the farm joyfully. I asked an explanation. Had he been talking to a medical convention, said he, he would have told them that the cancer had reversed itself; had he been asked the reason why, he would have said that someone had laid hands on her and prayed for her.

To those who say this case was psychosomatic, I must recount another case less easy to dismiss. My wife had hurt her spine and had occasion to seek treatment from a famous doctor with degrees in medicine and osteopathy. I saw this careful specialist exhibit x-ray photographs, before and after, of a boy whose diseased leg was shorter than his healthy one by seven centimeters. The first x-ray exposed the femurs diseased edge; the second showed the femur faultless and six centimeters longer than before. Viola Fryman then explained that she had no idea why the bone was still a centimeter shorter than the other one, but she suggested that it might be growing still. Could this be psychosomatic? No, the boy was not the one who prayed. After reading Kathryn Kuhlman's book, the mother prayed. Her's were the prayers that were answered. I saw the boy without his usual iron leg-support romp around the room.

But why are so ma y seekers after healing left unhealed? In friendly group encounter, I once asked a famous healing preacher why, in his or other healing ministries, just five percent or less of all going forward were reported healed, the others disappointed. He answered frankly: "I do not really know, but it keeps me humble."

It may rather be that Jesus Christ, being Deity incarnate, healed all who came to Him in faith; He gave healing gifts to His apostles, but their scope was limited, Epaphroditus being sick at Rome, and at Miletus so was Trophimus, the healing gift of Paul without effect. Sickness among saints today needs no recounting, for even healers suffer.

Some advocates of healing tell their following that if a Christian should remain unhealed it is because of unbelief or other sin within his heart. This doubtful doctrine does not match the facts of life. There are too many instances of godly folk who suffered pain with fortitude, yet radiated faith and hope and love until they died.

As healing is a gift for other's benefit, so also is the gift of power. One never reads in Sacred Writ of anyone who worked a miracle for his own benefit. Of course, too many folk are prone to claim "a miracle" in every happening of their lives. The current use of the word "miracle" is very cheap. The Spirit's gift, "dynamic" in the Greek, is never magic.

Likewise prophecy is meant for others' good, relaying messages from God to His own people, so often leading to conviction and conversion, to restoration and renewal, and to infilling of the Spirit. Prophecy is the anointed utterance, the empowered proclamation. It is the greatest of the gifts, the one that Paul urged saints to covet most (1 Corinthians 14:1-5). Prophecy is the great evangelistic gift and, in times of great revival, it is seen at best advantage in the great revivalists and great evangelists.

No doubt there are occasions where prophecy is given for the guidance of an individual, where the Scriptures could not offer help of any kind in circumstances peculiar to the need. But it is difficult to make comparison between prophetic utterance and medleys of Elizabethan phrases often passed for prophecy. The use of Shakespeare's words to give direction to the saints today is just as odd as Joseph Smith's ability to translate sentences in Reformed Egyptian into Elizabethan English.

And some ambitious speakers do not hesitate to put their own proposals forth to sound as if the Lord Himself had prompted them. Others feel that they must fix the dates for God's events. As is the case of hoaxes in general, it takes some time for them to be exposed.

The charismatic movement of the 1830's produced the Catholic Apostolic Church. The "gift of prophecy" was manipulated by determined men to set up an extravagantly liturgical ecclesi, and to get rid of Edward Irving himself, the leader of the movement. Most of the developments that marked the Catholic Apostolic Church off from other Churches, such as appointment of their Twelve Apostles and the clear prediction that the Lord would come before the last of them would die, were initiated by a calculated use of "prophecy." For a while, it seemed as if the charismatic movement of the 1970's was about to be manipulated by some similarly motivated men. Sometimes it has been amusing to observe.

An able charismatic leader told me once that when he visited a convention, he was made aware of others anxious to enlighten him on some disputed point. This they did by "using" prophecy. Speaking as God, first person singular, they offered kindly comment on his service for the Lord, then stated that he had much to learn if he would listen. And was my friend impressed? Not at all, said he. If it had been the Lord who gave the word, the Lord would surely know that he was not named Patrick; "Pat" was a nickname.

Discernment, tongues, interpretation: these three are mystery gifts. They cannot be explained or even analyzed. The Acts of the Apostles tell of Paul's discernment of the thoughts of evil men. Discernment was a feature of the work of Evan Roberts, known to tell an utter stranger in a meeting that his troubles had begun through forging someone's signature two years before.

No doubt, instances abound today of real discernment. An English-speaking evangelist found himself in Norway during the revival of the middle 1930's. He was baffled in the leadership of meetings because of language barriers. So he turned to God to seek the promise of discernment of the hearts of men. Long afterwards, he found discernment operating in his ministry, but only in those meetings where the presence of the Lord was strongly felt. Yet he was utterly unable to explain the workings of the gift; it was something that was "better felt than telt." Discernment of the thoughts of men appears to be a gift without a rational elucidation, not irrational but a-rational.

That stated, it is easier to deal with glossolalia, the gift of tongues, which does not mean (of course) linguistic skill. The gift of tongues, described in 1 Corinthians, appears to be an incomprehensible utterance of the Spirit speaking in a mystery to God, not the proclamation of the Gospel in the languages of men reported on the day of Pentecost and not again in any apostolic literature. This gift too could be described as an a-rational endowment. Its greatest benefit appears to be toward recipients themselves. What use is it? What good does it do? These are the usual questions, and those who claim to have the gift, who seem above reproach, declare the gift most edifying to themselves.

Enthusiastic people often give reports of instances where the language used in tongues turned out to be a language of a foreigner who happened in the meeting. In 1936, I heard of tongues used in a Californian church but recognized as Mandarin profanity or Hebrew of Davidic purity according to the critics point of view. I failed to find just who the speakers or the experts in the language were! So many claims appear to be by hearsay, and many wishful thinking. It seemed impossible to find a case were name and actual circumstances of the speaker or the hearer where available. Documented confirmation seemed to be extremely rare.

In a Pennsylvanian journal I noticed a report that in a church three thousand miles away, an utterance in tongues was taped and sent to linguists at the university, who said that "it was Basque." I asked the rector, a good friend of mine, for details. No, he had not exercised his gift on that occasion, but another did and it was taped, and several Nisei pastors thought it sounded like Chinese. Concluding that instances today are tongues that "no one understands" (1 Corinthians 14:2) does not make them less authentic.

It is understood that people persecuted for distinctive emphasis tend to exaggerate in making claims for it. So they are not content with general agreement on validity of gifts today, but must insist that glossolalia is the only or initial evidence of the filling of the Spirit, going far beyond the Scriptures in their claim, while ever blithely disregarding the experiences of many men of God whose Spirit-filled dynamic won general approval.

Intransigence like this has hindered progress in recovery of apostolic gifts, for it is nowhere clearly stated in the Scriptures, yet it is preached and practiced with a greater zeal than is employed in advocating clearly stated "fruit." Undoubtedly, the gift of tongues occurred among the Jews, Samaritans, and the Gentiles first as signs of their acceptance by the Lord. But there are instances where tongues were lacking. The purpose of the sign was recognition, and the need for such a sign depends upon the need for recognition.

The Holy Spirit has apportioned gifts to each one as He wills, therefore to insist upon the gift of

tongues presumes upon divine prerogatives. So advocates of the necessity of tongues have been compelled
to add the doctrine of "initial evidence of tongues" as
something quite distinct from any "gift of tongues"
about which so much advice is given, just as others
teach that the Spirit of God is quite distinct from the
Spirit of Christ, an unsubstantiated notion.

It is forgotten that this gift of tongues is
relegated by the Apostle Paul to a place of less
importance than the others, self-edifying only,
incomprehensible to the speaker unless interpreted,
confounding to outsiders, prone to extravagant
indulgence and leading to confusion unless safeguarded.
It is the only gift on which some limitations have been
placed.

Yet the Apostle claimed to speak in tongues
"more than you all." He urged Corinthians not to forbid
speaking in tongues, but to do it in decency and order,
and to covet the best gifts. That advice is good today.
The gift of tongues can be counterfeited. Furthermore,
outside of evangelical religion, there have been alien
tongues in alien religions.

Why should anyone attempt to fake tongues? If
nine young men were seeking to be filled, but each
one was resolved to speak in tongues and to refuse
another gift as evidence, the obvious outcome would be
nine young men, or possibly just eight, still tarrying
for their self-appointed evidence, and trying every
possible method of inducing the mysterious utterance.
And furthermore, as others of their friends have
already talked in tongues, genuine or not, they feel
that their continued lack of evidence is a reflection on
themselves. In despair, they are ready to try anything.
Who knows what trouble may ensue.

I heard a television personage advise all seekers
to repeat the sacred Name a thousand times so rapidly
that tongue-control would then be lost and glossolalia
result. I know of an evangelist exhorted to make up
the tongues along the way and take by faith as
tongues whatever he could utter! Mercifully, fanaticism
is declining in proportion to increase of interest in the

charismata in the churches.

Interpretation is also a mystery gift, a-rational, by which one listening to an utterance in tongues is moved to give interpretation, though he himself has failed to recognize a single word by any rational consideration. Interpretation also can be counterfeited, but the counterfeiting recognized.

A Pentecostal pastor told me how he and another pastor, born in Europe, tested the discernment of a congregation in Los Angeles. In an open meeting, the other pastor recited the Beatitudes in French and the Lord's Prayer in Dutch; an interpreter arose and gave as "interpretation" of these recitations something wholly unrelated to their content. There is no test for truth in tongues, other than a witness of the Spirit that something is amiss.

In these days of interest in the charismata, the gifts of the Spirit, it is widely assumed that manifestation of any one of the gifts is evidence that the one expressing such a gift is obviously and currently filled with the Spirit.

This is a clearly demonstrated fallacy and a very serious error. Take the gift of an evangelist. I once asked a dedicated layman in South Island, New Zealand, under whose ministry he had been converted. He mentioned an evangelist of great fame around the world in the 1920's. He must have noticed a shadow of regret upon my face, for he said: "I hear that he went wrong after that." I was most reluctant to let him know that the evangelist was sadly out of God's will at the moment of his conversion. This man had compromised his ministry in Britain by careless conduct with the other sex. In North America, he repeated his misconduct. So he left for faraway New Zealand, where the pastor of a leading congregation, doubting stories of his conduct, tried him out in his own Sunday services and convinced, hired the Auckland Town Hall for a city-wide campaign. And during that campaign, he was again exposed as a seducer.

God's gifts and callings are without a "change of mind" upon His part. Jonah, called to go to Nineveh, refused and boarded ship for the Mediterranean's farthest shore. His disobedience did not mean withdrawal of the call. Likewise, when God bestows a gift, He does not take it back again because the one receiving it is disobedient or exploitive.

Two family friends accosted me in the streets of Oxford, one remarking how sorry she felt because a certain healing preacher had died in California. I hesitated to tell her that he had died of acute alcoholism, a vice which he matched with his philandering. It seems that when he had visited London, our friend had "gone forward" for healing, and had been healed of the effects of polio; this we knew, for she formerly had walked with a damaged leg and now walked freely without a limp. It seemed sadly obvious that the preacher had been out of God's will during years of careless conduct, yet still exercised his gift of healing. Again, the only explanation seemed to be that the Lord who had given him this gift did not choose to take it back when His servant disobeyed and began to exploit his calling.

With this in mind, I once asked a pastor of a Pentecostal congregation whether he had ever heard a member exercise the gift of tongues to the congregation's satisfaction, then seriously backslide into sin but still try to exercise his gift in the meeting. Reluctantly, he told me that his church body had expelled a member who had been involved in calculated adultery but who still wished to exercise his glossolalia.

It seems to me that the gifts of the Spirit are weapons through which divine power is exercised. As soon as a soldier completes his basic training, he is taught the use of a weapon, whether a carbine, or a bazooka, or whatever. But the same soldier, disobeying commands, may use his weapon to rob a bank or to terrorize civilians. There have been far too many instances of charismatic servants of God who have disobeyed their Lord and abused their gifts. One tragic example may be found in the mass suicides in jungles of Guyana, an extreme example, without doubt.

All goes to show that exercise of a gift is not

evidence that the person concerned is currently committed to holy living and filled with the Holy Spirit.

How should this survey of the power and gifts be briefly summarized? The promise of the Lord to His disciples was power, and power is needed more than ever to achieve the purposes of God.

The greatest and most fruitful gifts are those of pastor, teacher and evangelist. The true evangelist persuades the uncommitted sinner to review his life, repent of sin, and be converted. He is the harvester. The pastor and the teacher make disciples of inquirers, and equip the saints for the work of ministering in the church and world. Show me a successful evangelist, or pastor, or teacher, and I will show you a man who made a full commitment of his life to God and sought the filling of His Spirit.

Today the churches need more power, not more schemes and gimmicks, not more organization and advertisement. "Not by might nor by power, but My Spirit," simply means "Not by organization nor by chain of command, but by My Spirit," according to the Hebrew.

We need the gifts of wisdom, knowledge, and faith. We need healing of the sick in mind and body. We need power to topple strongholds of the Evil One. We need anointed words of prophecy. We need discernment in these days of satanism. There is a proper place for tongues in worship, and for interpretation, subject to proper limitation.

But the charismata of the Spirit are not the greatest things; they are far inferior to love, the motivating force. And love is manifested in a nine-fold way, in love and joy and peace, in patience, kindness, goodness, in faithfulness, meekness and self-control. These are the fruit of the Spirit in the soul, these are the abiding evidence of a Spirit-filled heart. These collectively are most to be desired.

What is the connection between full commitment, decisive dedication, and the filling of the Spirit? Nowhere in the Scripture does it say: "O God, convert me;" it is "Repent and be converted." The sinner is asked to turn, to be converted. What does God do with a converted personality? He regenerates his life. Nowhere does a saint request: "O God, commit me;" the saint is told to dedicate decisively his life to God. What does God do with a committed life? He fills it with His Spirit.

# Chapter 18

## THE FRUIT OF THE SPIRIT

If the exercise of a gift is not abiding evidence of the fullness of the Spirit, what is? "But the fruit of the Spirit is love, joy, peace, patience, kindness, goodness, faithfulness, meekness, self-control; against such there is no law" (Galatians 5:22-23). The word "fruit" is a collective singular. The nine fruit of the Spirit must not be thought of as nine differing fruits, such as an apple, an orange, a pomegranate, and the like, but rather as a cluster of grapes on a single stem, for all nine fruit hang together, and not one without the other. When the believer evidences one, he evidences all.

When a Christian is filled with the Holy Spirit, his heart is full of love. He cannot help it. He is possessed of a love for God transcending anything he has hitherto known. And if his heart is full of love, it is likewise full of joy that is unspeakable, which has to be experienced to be appreciated. And if it is full of joy, it is full of peace that passes all understanding. These three fruit, love, joy, and peace, are primarily God-ward, although they produce the same kind of attitudes man-ward. Love is benevolent, and joy is expectant and peace is with contentment.

If a believer's heart is full of peace toward God, it is possessed of a profound patience towards his friends, his associates, and even his enemies. Once he has lost his patience with people, he has lost his peace with God. And patience bestows kindness, just as impatience provokes unkindness. And kindness gives way to real goodness. It is impossible for a believer to try to exercise patience with God, or to be kind to God, or to be good to God. These three fruit are primarily man-ward, to God's creatures.

The last three, faithfulness, meekness and self-control, are primarily self-ward, being effective in discipline, in humility, and in temperance. Their merits may be gauged by considering their opposites. No Spirit-filled believer is unreliable, arrogant, or undisciplined. Each of these three fruit is related to the other, and all three are related to the other expressions of the nine-fold fruit of the Spirit, expressions of love, the character of God.

The fruit of the Spirit is the real and immediate test of the abiding fullness of the Holy Spirit. A couple of missionaries, locked up in jail like Paul and Silas, have nothing in hand to demonstrate their power in soul-winning, but the fruit of the Spirit will enable them to sing praises at midnight, to remain in jail in order to reach a jailer, and to be ready in season and out of season with the Gospel.

The fruit of the Spirit is the abiding evidence of the filling of the Holy Spirit. A believer may be pleased to offer other evidence of his having received a great enduement of power from on high, such as the gift of prophecy or the gift of tongues, but the Apostle Paul made it clear that if anyone spoke with tongues of men or of angels, and yet showed no love he is was making a discordant noise. Paul cited no less than five of the gifts of the Spirit, not depreciating their value, but noting their inferiority to love. Clearly, love is the sum total of the fruit of the Spirit.

The fruit of the Spirit is the abiding evidence. As the gifts or callings of God are without repentance on His part, a believer may still be exercising an evangelistic or other gift after the power of the Spirit has departed from him, but not so with the fruit of the Spirit, which abides as long as the fullness of the

Spirit remains.

What actually is the filling of the Holy Spirit? Paul the Apostle, declared: "Do not get drunk with wine, for that is debauchery; but be filled with the Spirit" (Ephesians 5:18). In alcoholic intoxication, a man is possessed by an alien spirit: a quiet man becomes rowdy; a careful man becomes extravagant; a decent man becomes bestial; a cautious man becomes reckless; and folks excuse him, saying "He is not himself, he is intoxicated." The filling of the Holy Spirit is a kind of God-intoxication. It is not fanaticism but possession of the personality of a believer by the Holy Spirit of God, whereby his conduct becomes more Christlike.

Why then are some folk so reluctant to be filled? An interested pastor told me that he was actually scared of being filled with the Holy Spirit. Why? He said that he was afraid of what he might do. Such as what? Acting in a strange or a fanatical way! I told him that he was insulting Jesus Christ by accusing the Holy Spirit even obliquely of fanaticism. The Holy Spirit is referred to as the Spirit of Jesus, as the Spirit of Christ. As Christ was the perfect gentleman in all His earthly ministry, so the Spirit of Christ is the Spirit of all gentlemanliness. The pastor's words were as insulting to Christ as would be an observation by a minister that he was afraid to invite an evangelist and his wife to stay in his home in case the wife wrecked all the furniture!

How then, may one seek to receive the enduement of power from on high? Christ told His disciples, in the quiet conference following their request that He teach them to pray: "If you then, who are evil, know how to give good gifts to your children, how much more will the heavenly Father give the Holy Spirit to those who ask Him?" (Luke 11:13, cf. Matthew 7:11).

The Holy Spirit in His indwelling presence is the blessing that the believer receives automatically when he receives Christ as Saviour. I have never known of a case where an unregenerate man asked the Lord to give him the indwelling of the Holy Spirit, but rather

of instances where the sinner cried to God for
forgiveness or mercy or salvation or eternal life. The
words of our Lord seem not to refer to regeneration,
but to the enduement of power from on high, the
infilling of the Holy Spirit.

It was in this connection then that Christ said:
"Ask, and it will be given you; seek, and you will find;
knock, and it will be opened to you." The Greek tense
is clear: keep on asking, keep on seeking, keep on
knocking! An asking, seeking, knocking Christian will
soon find out for himself what stands in the way of
the filling of his vessel with the Holy Spirit, the clean,
righteous, convicting Spirit who hates sin and unrighteousness and compromise. The Holy Spirit will lead him
to seek forgiveness of his sins through the cleansing
blood of Christ, and to accept by faith His provision
for a victorious life, fully surrendering his life to God.
Then, by faith, and only by faith, the seeker may act
upon the promises of God, to receive into his most
unworthy vessel the mighty power of God the Spirit.

One thing is certain: God does not call the
unemployed to such a service. In Kimberley, a young
man told me of his great desire to know the filling of
the Spirit. I asked him what he was doing for the Lord
just then. He admitted that he was not very busy for
the Lord; he taught no class in Sunday School; he
shared in no evangelistic effort; he did little more than
go to Sunday services. I told him that he was like a
messenger boy asking for a car to do his work when
he was not even using the bicycle he had.

The busier a fellow gets, even working in his own
weak way, the more he comes to realize his need for
power; and sooner or later he will seek the source of
all the power and dedicate decisively his personality to
God. So dedication is the crucial act; the filling is the
work of God.

The test of this decisive dedication is simply
made: Is there some area of life remaining uncommitted? Is there a need of exercising faith? The faith
must rest upon God's promises, and none of them has
ever been revoked.

# Epilogue

I have hesitated much about the writing of an epilogue. But after seeking guidance and counsel of my friends, I felt that I should end this treatise on complete commitment with a private testimony, for at least two reasons: first, it is not thought improper for a convert to tell others of the doctrine of salvation and then to add his personal experience; second, there is not so much persuasion found in chapters on commitment if the writer has no testimony to offer thereupon. This said, I need not offer an apology for reference to my own personal affairs. Instead I pray that this witness may give credit only to the heavenly Father who gives good gifts to those who seek them for His glory.

My mother was the youngest daughter of a family living in the country district where the Irish 1859 Revival first appeared. She pointed me to Christ when I was but a lad of nine, on my ninth birthday in fact. I recall, for she held a theory that a youngster's heart will take impressions just like wax, but keep them just like marble. She believed implicitly that if a child was old enough to trust his mother, he was old enough to trust the Lord for his salvation.

Until I enrolled in courses at the College of Technology, Belfast, I had maintained a Christian testimony insofar as normal boys can be consistent. But at the "Tech", whose classes carried me to University of London entrance (or Junior College level in America), few of my friends could think of me as a believer. I did not swear or drink or even smoke or plunge into the grosser sins, but neither did I frequent prayer meetings or attend evangelistic services, except as family duty in the company of my mother or my immediate family.

Once, to my shame, a cousin of another faith rebuked me for my carelessness in conversation. Ashamed, I started taking interest more in spiritual affairs. Never having been baptized, I sought it in our church of family loyalty, the Baptist Church on Great Victoria Street, the down-town church of that denomination in Belfast, of which my second cousin David Henderson was minister. Earlier, when my father died in 1922 and left us orphans, this kindly church showed its consideration in a way that made me regard it all the more as the church of my boyhood.

Shortly after that, because of a girlfriend's influence, I started to attend the weekly meetings of the Young People's Society in the Cregagh Methodist Church. Here I found opportunity to engage in "Christian Endeavour." At this time I was also greatly influence by the writings of Mrs. Howard Taylor which interested me in the work of the China Inland Mission and in the principle of faith.

In this connection, while still a teenager, I met Ernest Hudson Taylor, son of the famous pioneer. He promised to pray for me daily. His letters were a challenge to my life, but I lost touch with him. Fifteen years or so passed and I was serving as chaplain in the South Pacific with the 13th U.S. Air Force. I was in London where he was dying in a ward in Mildmay Hospital. I visited there and he recognized me and we shared together the goodness of the Lord. I asked him: "Did you pray for me every day as promised?" For a moment I wished I had not asked him, for a shadow of regret fell on his face, but then he smiled again. "I must have missed you only six or seven days," he said. "Believe me the pain was very great those days." I turned away and wondered just how much I owed to that man's prayers. He died of cancer shortly afterwards.

These were the spiritual factors in my life when God gave me a call to preach, which I obeyed in the open-air in 1932, at just twenty years of age. I shared in Belfast's Youth Evangelistic Campaign, organized by many churches and their societies that year. The chief missioner was Lionel B. Fletcher, afterward a helpful friend. But more and more I found the literature of past revivals and awakenings moving my soul. Because of this, my friends and I, all younger men, formed a Revival Fellowship to pray for spiritual awakening around the world. We decided, wisely I believe, not to create a formal organization but to keep it as a loose fellowship. It lasted until World War II.

Until 1933, although I had so much for which to be thankful in my Christian experience, there were also sorry inconsistencies in my private life which brought me to despair, the kind of despair so graphically described in the seventh chapter of the Roman letter. In August 1933, although our Fellowship was at its peak of usefulness in Ulster at the time, I felt a pressing need for a deeper spiritual experience. So I turned to an associate whom I regarded as more spiritual than I could claim to be, Charles Coulter, who was reckoned to be a man of prayer. Coulter like me was baffled by conflicting teachings of so many schools of thought on sanctification and the Holy Spirit, but he was more specific in his views than I, for he possessed Salvation Army convictions. I was most uncertain in my mind, but in my heart was convinced that God, who had delivered from the guilt of sin, must have made provision to deliver from the power of sin also.

Hence, upon a Monday night, the 14th day of August 1933, Charles and I met with an Englishman who served a Belfast congregation. Pastor Rudkin gladly gave up his one evening off to talk with two young Irishmen about the deeper life. At ten o'clock that night, my mental grasp of the way of full surrender was as clear as the hunger in my heart for it. I disagreed with Mr. Rudkin on terminology but did

not worry much about mere words. The clock struck
ten as J. J. Morgan, senior minister, entered the room
suggesting tactfully an adjournment of discussion. It
was just as I was asking Rudkin: "Then what hinders
me being surrendered and filled for service?" So we
knelt to pray.

This was the first occasion in my life when I felt
assured in heart that God was talking to me. It was
not with a voice heard by my ears, but through the
indwelling Holy Spirit. I well remember praying, vowing
to God that I was willing to do anything, anything to
be surrendered and infilled. The others prayed in turn,
but I hold no recollection of anything they said. The
inner Voice was asking: "What about your own besetting sins?"

My own besetting sins? I hated them, I loathed
them, and willingly confessed them. I promised to
forsake them. This did not seem to be the problem, for
I knew that Jesus' blood was fully efficacious to
cleanse away all sins confessed to God. The Voice was
asking: "What about your will?"

That came as a new thought to me. I recalled
that I was undertaking correspondence courses with the
China Inland Mission with a view to becoming a missionary candidate as soon as my mother was provided
for, so I responded gladly that I was willing to be a
missionary anywhere, or to remain at home, or enter
full-time ministry, or stay in business. I felt rather
pleased that I was so willing!

Then God's Spirit spoke to me about an idol in
my life, a love affair, and asked me whether I was
willing if God so required, to give it up. I suddenly
became aware that I was not willing, but instead of
saying so I tried pretending that I was. In other
words, I was willing to do anything for God provided
that I could have my way in matters of the heart.

A working father was called home to meet a little
family crisis. Six-year-old Johnny had wedged his fist
within a precious Chinese vase. The mother and the
doctor wanted dad's permission to break the vase. "Not
at all," said the exasperated father, who remembered

what the vase was worth. Neither olive oil nor icy water helped a bit, so the mother pointed out that Johnny could not go through life with a vase implanted on his hand. Reluctantly, the father gave consent to use a hammer. At that point, young Johnny asked if it would help were he to drop his penny. The little rascal had been willing to let his parents smash a work of art in order that he might keep his grubby little fist around his precious penny which he had dropped within the priceless vase.

I too was willing then to let the heavenly Father smash the vessel He had fashioned for my life, in order just to keep my fist on an adolescent love affair. I was determined never to let go, and so I argued. God's Spirit left off speaking to my soul; my heart grew cold, so cold that I was frightened. The hungering for God returned, and I let go: "Not my will, but thine be done." I committed all my life to God, including unsurrendered areas of will. Then I simply took the promises by faith, and thanked the Lord.

I would be no more willing to describe in detail all that followed than a gentleman would think of telling strangers of his honeymoon. But I can say my heart was overwhelmed with love and joy and peace unspeakable, too great to bear. And this was noticed by my friends, whom I had by then forgotten. We did not terminate our prayers until after two next morning. For the first time in my life I felt that I really knew my God and Saviour, that Christianity itself was more than a philosophy or way of teaching or believing. I felt that impact in my mind and will and heart. The memory of those hours is always precious to my soul.

With happy steps I walked on home. "To walk" was not the word, for I ran down the street much like a messenger with a good-news telegram; at three o'clock, I found myself kneeling by the rocking-chair in the kitchen, trying to pray softly so that my light-sleeping mother upstairs would not hear me. Then all the sunshine was interrupted by a cloud, for I was reminded of some petty sums of money I had stolen from my mother's purse so many years before. I promised to confess it, and found that I was walking in the light once more.

Next morning, Mother asked what time I had come home the night before. I could have equivocated by fifty-five minutes from force of habit, and I felt like keeping silence to avoid discussing private, spiritual affairs with one of my own family, something always difficult for me. But on reflection, I decided that if my experience was real, I had nothing to conceal. So I briefly told her why we two had stayed up late. I expected her to tell me of her pious hopes for an improvement in my character and conduct. Instead, tears came to her eyes, something I seldom saw.

It seemed that she had waited for a blessing in a meeting of Faith Mission workers, seeking full sur-render and the filling of the Spirit, more than twenty-one years before. Disappointed that the Lord had not seen fit to call her to unusual service after that, she comforted herself, while caring for a dying husband and raising several children as a widow, by hoping that the Lord would claim her unborn child, born shortly afterwards.

Within one month, the love affair was terminated by the other partner, and I was asked to join the staff of a London based society, and so resigned my job. Disappointed at the start by cancellation of the London call, I placed my trust in God and started out with only half-a-crown (or half a dollar) to travel round the world to urge believers everywhere to pray and to prepare for a worldwide awakening.

Thus began my earliest stage of ministry, when for two years, I undertook apprenticeship in the life of faith and during the Depression lived from hand to mouth, from Land's End in England to John O'Groats in Scotland, from Lisbon to Leningrad, from Oslo to Jerusalem. I told the story in three travel books whose final chapters gave the message of those days: "Full Surrender," "The Price of Revival," and "The Filling of the Holy Spirit."

The second stage of ministry began in September

1935, when I left to tour the British Commonwealth and the United States of America. Occasionally, in Canada and the States, I saw revivals of intensity, the fruits of which continue to this day, as others will agree. The same was true of places in New Zealand, in Australia, and in South Africa. The ministry was first directed to believers, and the results occurred among believers. Nevertheless, there were approximately ten thousand professions of conversion within a single year. I would not think of claiming that these ten thousand inquirers persevered, but encounters with the converts on the mission fields, in ministry, lay witness, and the like, lead me to think that the rate of perseverance was not less than that of popular evangelism. At the end of this period, lacking guidance, I went off to Lapland just to pray. One outcome was a happiness in marriage unsurpassed by anyone within my ken.

Then came a period of decline. In my own strength, I took a team of seven to Australia, tackling all the lesser towns and cities in evangelism. Perhaps a thousand converts to the faith were made, but there was less of blessing in six months with seven workers than there had been in six weeks alone two years before. I afterward discovered that there had been serious scandal in the life of more than one, but the less said about it the better.

During this time, the ministry to which God called me was neglected: revival, individual and collective. Instead I concentrated on direct evangelism. I can only say that God was not with me in power; but neither was I conscious of disobedience in my life. The warmth of interest in the work of quickening believers and reviving congregations had declined, and there was limited success in repeating tactics of an earlier time but without the power.

My association in Toronto with the missionary pastor, Oswald J. Smith, was one of fruitful blessing. In 1940, I felt compelled to go and study once again. The purpose of five years of study may be gauged by topics chosen for a Th.D. dissertation at Northern

Baptist Seminary in Chicago and the D.Phil. thesis at the University of Oxford: histories of great awakenings, 1858 in North America and 1859 in Britain respectively. These pursuits were interrupted by three years or so of military service as an Air Force chaplain in World War II in the Pacific, in which the Lord blessed evangelism of an apologetic sort to high school graduates and university men with whom I served, not revival, but a very blessed military evangelism, reported officially in war histories.

During the years of dearth, I enjoyed the friendship of a man of God of my own age. I had shared a burden for revival with two older folks, Mrs. Henry Woods of New Jersey and Dr. Ernest Wadsworth of Chicago, but at the time, few believed in the possibility of true revival. But God raised up a friend who never ceased reminding me of my own original call. Armin Richard Gesswein, who as a Lutheran pastor, started writing me about the prospects for revival and who in 1937 saw real revival in Norway. He kept talking to me about it, causing me to rake the embers of my interest in revival and the deeper life.

In Oxford, during my researches, interest in revival or awakening grew within my heart as I was reading stories of God's wondrous doings in the past. American evangelists, learning that I was in Oxford, started making pilgrimages to my home in Wolvercote. To all of them I talked about revival. Several spent a day discussing expectations of revival in this modern age. I began to pray that if the Lord no longer used me, other than to write the message, He would use me to pass on the burden to these younger men. One in particular was Billy Graham.

In 1948 in London, I sat listening one day to the secretary of the Keswick Convention, Andrew Mac-Beath, who had witnessed real revival in the Congo. He told a striking story of a visitor to France who used to have his quiet time in a tiny Roman Catholic parish church. The British visitor had noticed that a middle-aged lady used to come each morning, promptly kneeling at the "stations of the Cross," then spending

half an hour in adoration of a lovely picture of the
Virgin Mary. The visitor commented on her great
devotion, but the parish priest told him reluctantly
that, thirty years before, the lady posed for a Parisian
artist's picture of the Virgin, and that she was only
contemplating what a beauty she had once imagined
herself to be.

That story stung me, for at that time I loved
recalling days when I received attention as a worldwide
evangelist in 1935 and 1936. One upshot was that I
began to pray that God would give me something to be
grateful for in 1949. My burden for revival and the
filling of the Spirit was renewed. I graduated from
Oxford and moved to California.

As 1949 began, Gesswein and I teamed up in a
minister's retreat near Minneapolis and saw a real
outpouring of the Holy Spirit, a forerunner of awakening among ministers in North America. In March of
1949 we shared ministry again, this time before four
hundred ministers, evangelists, missionaries, and their
wives, meeting for protracted prayer for revival in Los
Angeles. Again a great outpouring of the Spirit, the
real turning point in the awakening in Southern
California occurred. Within six months, the City of the
Angels saw the greatest evangelistic campaign of a
generation, under Billy Graham's anointed preaching.

At the 1949 prayer meetings in Los Angeles, a
prophecy was given that a movement would soon begin
in Minnesota. In April, such an outbreak of revival
started in St. Paul, on Bethel College campus, where
narration of revival history and teaching on the deeper
life resulted in profound revival. Perhaps this Minnesota student work began at midnight in a meeting of
committed men in Billy Graham's office. So I stirred up
the gift and preached essentials of revival and the way
of full commitment. Awakenings in the colleges
continued for a year or more.

It was at the Student Briefing Conference at
Forest Home in the San Bernardino Mountains of
Southern California that I shared ministry with Billy
Graham again. We talked each day about the topics of

the day, the topics of this book. The conversation of evangelists, like that of other professional people, is very much a comparing of notes or discussing of incidents peculiar to the life of evangelists. But this was not the case with Billy Graham discussing the awakenings or the deeper life. The climax of our talks occurred just after midnight Wednesday night, when he told me of his great desire for renewal of his consecration and anointing of the Holy Spirit.

Two hours after midnight he came back to my cabin and told me that he had received not only the much sought-for blessing but also an assurance that he was going to see a real revival in his campaign in downtown Los Angeles. The Graham Crusade made history, and his ministry began to change from good to better. I heard him preach to many thousands on the filling of the Holy Spirit, not a common topic in the 1950's. I thanked God for answered prayer.

Following that time I sought out evangelists, especially the younger men, and talked to them fraternally about the great enduement of power from on high. I scarcely ever knew one to be indifferent. Some talked until two or three o'clock in the middle of the night. Sometimes I had such a burden for them that I prayed until dawn about it. All of them requested details of the message, Scripture references and the like, until I reached a point where I was willing, if I had only a month to live, to spend it writing down the message, and that is how this present work was written.

In 1952, an opportunity was given to address the message to the churches of a nation. Throughout Brazil, the Holy Spirit took the Word and stirred the churches up to seek revival. The American Bible Society reported (1952) that "time and time again, the largest auditoriums could not seat the thousands who came to hear the Gospel." The Evangelical Confederation's published report noted: "Noteworthy in the 1952 Revival were churches that were crowded for prayer at 6 o'clock in the morning." The Presbyterian Church (U.S.A.) spoke of "a deep and widespread spiritual revival in the churches and thousands of conversions." The messages were published as "Plena Submissao."

Ten years later, I addressed a conference of clergy in England on the subject of commitment and the filling of the Spirit. An Anglican minister wrote a year later about the "clear and reasonable presentation of the doctrine of the Holy Spirit," adding that "last month, the Spirit broke dramatically into my life . . . I have been a changed person ever since and so has my beloved wife. The signs were perfect love to God and men; perfect peace; continuous joy; much fruit; abundant life; power; wisdom; in fact, every blessing in Christ Jesus and all the glory His . . . My reasons for writing are to encourage you personally and to ask your prayer support." He was not the only one there present soon to embark upon a worldwide ministry.

The message is a simple one. Our blessed Saviour not only made provision that His children might be delivered from the guilt of sin, by faith, but also showed a clearly stated way whereby shortcomings of His children might be confessed, forgiven. and cleansed at any time. His message also taught that obedient Christians may claim by faith a victory over sin, enter upon a closer walk with God, fully committing their lives to God, and be filled with the Spirit for whatever service He may direct.

This book is sent out, therefore, with the prayers of many, as well as of the author, that it may encourage the reviving of the spiritual experiences of pastors, evangelists, teachers, ordinary church members, new converts, and others whom the Lord may choose to bless.